Routledge Revivals

New Enterprises

A constant growth of new small firms is an important part of a healthy economy, yet little is known about the factors which determine success or failure in a small business. Success is concerned not only with the development of a product and its market but, more importantly, with the individual behind it. There are very few completely new ideas or products to guarantee success; therefore, the person seeking to start their own business must assemble customers and resources themselves before they start trading. The cases outlined here are all based on actual experience, and explore the issues and problems facing would-be entrepreneurs. They offer step-by-step advice on the processes involved in starting a small business and demonstrate the wide range of business opportunities available. First published in 1982, this is a detailed and practical guide, particularly applicable to those who find the idea of establishing a small business of their own appealing.

New Enterprises

A Start-Up Case Book

Sue Birley

Routledge
Taylor & Francis Group

First published in 1982
by Croom Helm Ltd

This edition first published in 2013 by Routledge
2 Park Square, Milton Park, Abingdon, Oxon, OX14 4RN

Simultaneously published in the USA and Canada
by Routledge
711 Third Avenue, New York, NY 10017

Routledge is an imprint of the Taylor & Francis Group, an informa business

Publisher's Note
The publisher has gone to great lengths to ensure the quality of this reprint but
points out that some imperfections in the original copies may be apparent.

Disclaimer
The publisher has made every effort to trace copyright holders and welcomes
correspondence from those they have been unable to contact.

A Library of Congress record exists under LC control number: 82194563

ISBN 13: 978-0-415-85836-6 (hbk)
ISBN 13: 978-0-203-79532-3 (ebk)
ISBN 13: 978-0-415-70279-9 (pbk)

New Enterprises:

A Start-Up Case Book

Sue Birley

CROOM HELM
London & Canberra

©1982 Sue Birley
Croom Helm Ltd, 2-10 St John's Road, London SW11

British Library Cataloguing in Publication Data

Birley, Sue
    New enterprises.
    1. Small business – Great Britain
    I. Title
    338.6'42'0941   HG3729.G7

ISBN 0-7099-0614-5
ISBN 0-7099-0680-3 Pbk

Printed and bound in Great Britain by
Biddles Ltd, Guildford and King's Lynn

CONTENTS

ACKNOWLEDGEMENTS

There are so many people who have contributed to my understanding of the start-up process, albeit sometimes involuntarily! I would like to thank particularly, however, those who have helped me to evolve this book. The contributors come top of the list. They have allowed me to share in, and report on, a very personal experience: their expectations and hopes as well as their mistakes.

I began collecting the cases for the book whilst Director of the New Enterprise Programmes and I would like to take this opportunity to thank all those who contributed to the success of a most exciting series of courses: including Paul Carradine and Charles Napier from Man-Power Services Commission; the tutors, Peter Wilson, Phil Dowell, Tony Marshall and Colin Wood; the programme secretary, Ann Clapp; and Sue Coan, the Registrar, without whom nothing would ever have happened.

I believe that in a new business there is no way of distinguishing the person and the business, and consequently the best way to understand the start-up process is to listen to, and to see, the entrepreneur himself. The best medium for this purpose is a combination of written case and film. Six of the cases have, therefore, been extended into a film also entitled 'New Enterprises'. I would like to thank Robert Smith and Sue Palmer from ICFC for suggesting two of the cases and for believing in my idea sufficiently to sponsor the film. It was made by a small firm, Molinaire, and produced by John Slater of Mirageland, who bullied me with style.

Janice Martin has been my secretary for the past two years and has patiently typed, corrected and assembled the manuscript — more than that, she has tolerated and organised me.

Finally there is my husband, colleague and friend, David Norburn, who nagged me into writing the book and who has always believed in what I have been trying to do in this much misunderstood world of the small firm.

INTRODUCTION

A steady supply of new small firms is an important part of a healthy economy, either as a source of self-employment, as a service to companies and to the community, or as the 'seed-bed' for the future. Despite this, little is known by academics, business, or government about the factors which determine success or failure, due in large part to the fact that the determinants are difficult to quantify and therefore forecast.

Success is concerned not only with the development of a product and its market-place, but more importantly with the individual. There are very few completely new ideas or products. Most new businesses are based upon redefining already-established market segments, or upon offering better products or services than those offered by established firms in existing markets. Accepting this, the person seeking to start his own business must not only assemble both customers and resources, but in doing so he must also establish some form of credibility before he is able to start trading: credibility with customers who may see themselves as taking unnecessary risks; credibility, and thus credit, with suppliers; and, of course, credibility with the bank. To succeed in starting, therefore, he must have energy, determination and some measure of realism as well as knowledge of the product and its market. But most of all, he needs luck.

This case-book is about such people and their ideas. It is intended for all those interested in or involved in the start-up process. Broadly, this can be divided into four main groups. First, there are the potential entrepreneurs themselves, who are seeking to learn about the issues and problems confronted by others. Secondly, there is the increasing group of professional advisors, who are concerned to steer their clients along the safest route. This group includes not only the traditional advisors, such as accountants and solicitors, but also the growing list of academics, government agencies and voluntary groups anxious to help the small firm sector in general and the start-up process in particular. Thirdly, there are the investors who are being asked to commit resources to an idea in embryo. This group includes not only the bank manager but any supplier who, by giving credit, is investing in the business. The last group are students: students of business management, in the professions, in the arts or sciences; any student who may one day fall into one of the above categories.

Starting a business is not a discrete event. It involves a series of decisions, some planned, some unplanned, which may take place over many years, prior to the establishment of a full-time trading company. This book is concerned with exploring the issues and problems facing all entrepreneurs during this process. All the cases and the people are real. Some are now established, healthy businesses; some have still to get off the ground. Some people have abandoned the idea as inviable and have started other businesses; some have returned to full-time employment. These are the results of the natural selection process. But what about the process itself?

The process by which new businesses are finally born is complex, since it involves personal decisions on the part of the entrepreneur as well as a series of chance events or 'triggers'. Equally, the timescale can be long or short according to the energy and motivation of the individual as well as the current economic environment. Six stages are usually experienced during the process:

Stage 1: Skill or interest developed

Obviously all individuals develop skills and interests in a number of ways. It can be through professional training, through practical work experience or through actively pursuing some leisure activity. It may be a manufacturing capability, selling skills or even an eye for a good product or deal.

Stage 2: Interest focused upon a product or market niche

Through the development of these skills individuals are constantly saying to themselves 'I could do that better' – and some begin to pursue one of their ideas, either through tentative discussion with family and friends, by designing the 'better mousetrap' on paper, or even by developing the first tentative prototypes or samples. At this stage, there is not necessarily any intention to convert the idea into a business. Nevertheless, the motivations will vary. Some will be interested to develop the product, quite apart from any market considerations. Indeed, the perpetual inventor or engineer enjoys the challenge of constantly creating new products and is unlikely ever to translate any into a business idea. Some will be concerned to find a product or develop a service idea which fits an identifiable gap in a market. Many of these ideas are based on the frustration of the individual unable, for example, to buy large size shoes, find a plumber to unblock his house drains, buy real ale in his locality, or find a printer who will deal in small quantities rapidly.

Stage 3: Interest formulated into a business idea

It is at this stage that the individual begins to translate an interest in a product or service into the basis for a business. The triggers for such a change can vary. Some are negative, such as enforced redundancy or other forms of personal rejection either at home or at work. Some are positive, such as an increasing belief in the viability of the idea, a need to be in control of individual destiny, or encouragement from friends and colleagues.

Many people, however, may not have a viable new business idea but may still wish to find a business which will allow them to escape from the perceived traps of employment. Such people often end up purchasing or setting up a newsagent or grocer's shop – the proverbial tiny business. Others may be tempted by the perceived lower risks of the purchase of a franchise.

Stage 4: First product or service sold part-time

We do not know the size of the black economy, nor do we know what proportion choose to remain within it and what proportion use it as a test-bed. However, it is clear that whether intending to defraud the taxman or not, many businesses are first piloted in the black or cash economy: professionals and skilled workers offering their services out of the firm's time at cheaper rates; products sold on market stalls or at craft fairs one day a week; goods customised for friends or neighbours in the home workshop and for payment in kind. All these are necessary test-markets for a large number of small businesses. As with all the other stages, many stop here, either because they begin to receive too many negative signals or because it is already sufficiently rewarding.

Stage 5: Full-time self-employment

For many the move to full-time self-employment or to freelancing can be a traumatic experience, particularly if it is accompanied by the rejection of a redundancy notice. The familiar support systems are no longer available and new, possibly less reliable, ones must be created. For others it is a blessed relief. For actors, artists and some professionals it is a normal way of life. Indeed many will have experienced no other.

Stage 6: Full-time business

The distinction between these last two stages is often blurred. Indeed, self-employment is by no means a necessary step to the formation of a business which directly employs more than one individual either full-time or part-time. Nevertheless, a *business* can be said to be formed when it has supplied and invoiced customers and when people in addition to the owners receive income from it.

Figure I.1: The Six Stages in the Start-up Process

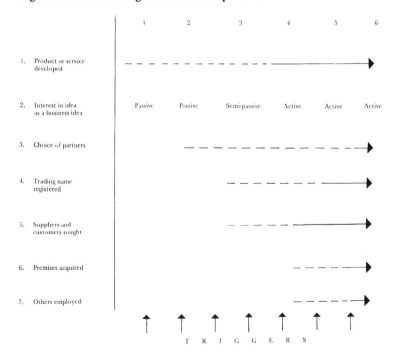

The six stages just described are shown in Figure I.1. They do not all take equal lengths of time, and sometimes they overlap. Nevertheless they do illustrate the peculiar nature of business formation. What should be emphasised, however, is that the successful launch of a business, whether or not it survives, requires the entrepreneur to convince others. It needs suppliers of raw materials, space, money, as well as customers to commit themselves to an individual, and an idea. If either the individual or his idea is not sufficiently strong, he will find it difficult to break the closed loop of the customer who will give an order when manufacturing facilities are set up and the banker who will only lend the money for premises, plant and equipment on the basis of a firm order.

In studying the start-up phase, three ingredients are essential: the right *person* with the right *product* put together in the form of the right *project*. So, in understanding success or failure we must ask:

- Does the person have the skills, goals and values that are both consistent with the proposed idea and are realistic? If not is it likely that he would be persuaded to change either by circumstances or colleagues?
- Is the product or service likely to be a strong enough base for an independent business, or would it be better as part of a complete line in another, already existing, business?
- Does the project make sense? Would it be better, for example, first to establish sales and to subcontract manufacture before putting down plant? Are the market forecasts and the marketing strategy realistic within the time scale suggested?

All these judgements are subjective. There are no formulae to help us to pick winners, but there are some guidelines, based upon experience. This case book aims to improve diagnostic skills, highlight the important questions and develop experience.

The Cases

Not all businesses which complete the process previously described grow to become medium sized and then large. Some are acquired by other, usually larger, companies along the way. But in a large proportion of cases the owner wishes to retain autonomy and control and his resultant style mitigates against moving from being small to medium sized. Many other companies fail to grow and eventually die, either because the owner lacks the skills needed to adapt his management style to the needs of a changing organisation or because the company encounters adverse market conditions.

At the time of writing, we do not know the eventual fate of the businesses described. Nevertheless, the cases cover companies at all stages in the start-up process, although there is a concentration upon businesses in the latter, more tangible stages. Some of the businesses will inevitably remain small, whilst some have the potential for massive growth. Some products lend themselves easily to start-up, some would fit more easily into an existing product line.

The book starts with a dream. Alan Sealey is a skilled turner unhappy with the way British engineering companies are run. Indeed the 'I could do better' syndrome, characteristic of many start-ups, also runs through cases like Continental Trucking, Independent Engineering Enterprises and Lingua Franca.

Much available data on failure suggests that a major contributing factor is the choice of partner. In many cases, this is a natural process, involving husband and wife; for others it arises out of a previous working relationship, as in Light Engineering, The Box, Eurobond Laminates or SFL. For all the question which arises is whether this is a satisfactory basis for a business relationship.

In general terms, the barriers to entry, as measured by financial needs, tend to be lower in service businesses or in businesses where it is possible to source manufacture whilst testing the market. Lingua Franca, Leather Imports and Girogift are in the former category, whilst the strategy which Colin Goss for Precision Engineering Industries proposes would fall in the latter.

Equally, a skill in handling supplies or markets overseas naturally points towards some form of import/export business. N & Z European Hi-fi relies upon the market knowledge and interest of two Yugoslavians unable to buy equipment easily. Leather Imports arises out of an apparently cheap source of supply through a relative in India.

Some products or ideas do not necessarily form the basis of a business, but rather a one-off deal. John Clark is offered a billion buttons for £1,000, an offer not to be missed − or is it? Hindle Engineering proposes a joint venture with a marketing organisation to manufacture aerosol fire-extinguishers. But, does the proposed deal make sense for a small subcontract engineering firm?

New products for existing markets are difficult to spot and to market. How does Malise Graham price his growing bag containers when there is no other obvious competition for comparison. For David Jones, the problem is two-fold. He must first decide what type of outlets are most appropriate for his omniclock before he is able to market price it.

Few entrepreneurs are in the enviable position of Tom Wills or Pam Murphy. Both have more than one product to offer to vastly different markets. Tom has made his choice. He will manufacture and market brake pads. But does his strategy make sense in the face of the nature and size of the competition? Will his product be so special as to overcome the obvious resistance from both competition and customers? Would he be better to start with the second stage of his strategy and set up a research company to develop the many new products and processes he has worked on? Pam Murphy has two problems. First, how many Slurrimasters should she order in the first batch from her fabricator, and second what arrangement should she make over Cowpact, an already proven product?

The last two cases in the book demonstrate a special type of new firm. In both cases, a trading entity has existed previously but with different ownership. Bob Kent and Patrick Thorpe have approached ICFC with a proposal to acquire the firm in which they are employed from its absentee owner. Malcolm Evans returns from holiday to find the resignations of his two partners awaiting him. For Bob, Patrick and Malcolm, a decision to continue with their companies will require a substantial change in their management style, at a time of trading difficulty for the firm.

Using the Book

This book is intended to be used by people who wish to learn about the process and problems involved in deciding whether a viable business can be formed from an idea. For some this may be to improve their analytical skills as investor, advisor or customer and for others to help them evaluate their own business idea through all its stages of development.

The cases have been arranged in the sequence described earlier in this chapter providing a complete course and so move from the half-formed ideas of Alan Sealey to the many possible businesses of Pam Murphy. Throughout it deals with people and their ideas. Some will succeed through sheer determination, others in spite of themselves. Some wish to grow, and maybe create monuments for the future, others are determined to stay small and in complete control of their own destiny. For all the question is whether they can realise their personal goals through the medium of the particular business idea explored. In studying and evaluating the start-up process, therefore, this must be the major question constantly in the mind of the reader. To answer this question, whether in the classroom or privately, the following three themes are suggested.

First, in order to help the reader focus his thinking, specific problems are posed at the end of each case. They are not exclusive but are intended as the basis from which general issues or problems should emerge.

The second theme concerns the fit between the person and the project. Unfortunately, however, all the information necessary to make such a judgement is rarely available. Either the entrepreneur does not know, does not wish to reveal all, or is simply unaware of its importance. Nevertheless, the reader must take a view on the potential of the idea at whatever stage he meets it. The following questions are suggested as a second theme which would run through all discussions.

From the information available, do the person and the project fit?
— If so, can the project be re-arranged to form a viable business?
— If so, does the person have the necessary skills?
— If not, what help is needed?

The third theme concerns the reader or student himself. We cannot give formulae for picking winners accurately — if we could, there would be many more healthy businesses as well as wealthy investors. Equally, we cannot legislate against the entrepreneur who is determined to proceed with an idea that will clearly fail, nor against the customer or banker who cannot see that 'this time it *will* work'. We can, however, improve skills and soften prejudices. In evaluating these businesses, it is as important for the reader to understand his own attitudes and prejudices as it is those of the case he is studying. Therefore, the third theme should question what factors in the reader's own experience and training have contributed to the particular conclusion he has arrived at. Does he lean more to numerical analysis than description? Does he always search for a particular level of education in the entrepreneur? Does he have fixed ideas about certain products or industries? Are certain types of personalities attractive to him? It is these questions, woven into discussion, which can make the study of start-up a rich educational experience for all.

Picking Winners

Although the book forms a complete course, it may be that time is short and the teacher merely wishes to introduce the area of 'start-up' to a group of managers. Picking Winners is an enjoyable way of achieving this. The group is presented with a number of cases, six being the optimum, and in syndicates asked to form a set of criteria for picking winners and then apply them to the six cases. The questions which the teacher might ask are, for example:

— Is there a business here?
— Does it need money?
— Would you invest in it?

The exercise will demonstrate the difficulties in forming rigid criteria and will highlight the problem of deciding how much information is actually needed at each stage in the investment decision process. Indeed, the private reader may also find this an enjoyable way of monitoring his own thoughts.

Translating the Dream into a Business

Entrepreneurs who are totally involved in the development of their business carry their business plan around in their heads. They argue frequently that since the idea is constantly changing as new information comes to light, it would be pointless to write it down. This also, of course, has the value of allowing them, albeit possibly unwittingly, to 'ignore' potential problems!

A business plan is a way of imposing discipline upon the process of formulating the business as well as eventually managing it. It should not be written once on tablets of stone but should be adapted to changing circumstances. A well-written plan does not need to be of great length but will form the basis of any discussion with investors or bankers. The last chapter of this book, therefore, is not a case study but a set of disciplined guidelines for those students who are at the point of finally translating a dream into reality.

1 THE DREAM: SEAMACH ENGINEERING*

Case A

In April 1979, Alan Sealey felt that he was finally in a position to leave his present employer and start the first phase to set up his own company which would offer sub-contract machining facilities to the engineering industry. This case outlines his thoughts at that time.

It has been my ambition to start my own company for a number of years, and I have spent these past years trying to accumulate sufficient capital to launch such an operation.

Having left school just before the age of 16, I served an apprenticeship as a turner in a small engineering company in Bath. I was employed in a medium-to-heavy engineering environment and involved in the manufacture of pumps, dockside cranes, deck machinery, construction equipment and, more recently, the offshore cranes used on oil rigs in the North Sea.

Throughout my apprenticeship I attended day-release classes at the local technical college where I gained a craft certificate to City and Guilds standard (passed with credit), but by the end of my apprenticeship I had become disillusioned about my future prospects. Though I enjoyed turning as a job, it was obvious to me that I would never get full satisfaction from it whilst working for someone else. I had my own ideas on the best way to run a machining operation and the type of equipment required to be successful, which were different from those of the companies I worked for. Perhaps the best way of giving you an idea of my opinions regarding areas for improvement in engineering today is to show you an article (see Appendix 1.3) from the *Guardian* which was based on an interview which I gave over the telephone as a result of a letter I had published in *The Financial Times*.

As I knew of nobody who would be in a position to finance me I had to rely on my own capacity to save. The best option open to me at that time appeared to be the merchant navy, and so I joined Shell Tankers (UK) Ltd, as a fifth engineer. I stayed with them for just over twelve months. However the job was too career-structured to enable me

*This case was written by Sue Birley from material provided by Alan Sealey.

to make any money in the short term and I also felt too far removed from the manufacturing environment to which I had become accustomed.

Having left Shell Tankers in 1975, I returned to my previous employer who in the meantime had started a nightshift in the machine shop. This seemed to offer me the opportunity of building up my capital base and so I started on the nightshift as a turner in May 1975 and soon gained the top skilled rate as a turner. Indeed, I was the youngest skilled turner to be in that position. I also increased my saving power where possible by investing on the Stock Exchange with which I had some success.

I have now served a four-year period of nights, and it is obvious to me that the method of running the machine shop has deteriorated still further and that the waste of resources, both manpower and machines, is something that I cannot work with any longer. Though I voiced my opinions to management in what I consider to be a constructive attitude, I have been unable to obtain any satisfaction whatsoever and now face the prospect that I may become thought of as a professional moaner. It is under these conditions that I am considering the offer of two friends to go into partnership as property developers. We bought a cottage at the beginning of 1979 and spend weekends and evenings renovating it. However, it is a very slow process and I feel that if I were to work full time on the project, by the autumn we would be able to sell the cottage and I would have enough capital to start my machining business.

Unfortunately the capital which I will have (about £7,000) will not be enough for my original intention which was to base my machining facility on the new generation of CNC [Computer Numerically Controlled] machine tools. Perhaps I should explain the relevance of machine tools in engineering. It is probably best summed up by saying that the machine tool is to engineering what the loom is to textiles. By the new generation of machine tools I refer to machines that are completely programmable for particular jobs. Rather than being controlled by an operator they are run by a pre-programmed tape via a control centre which for all intents and purposes is a computer. It is possible to run each tape through each machine's individual control system or run a number of machines from one central control. These machines are being developed on a continuing bases with the advent of the micro-chip. They offer great advantages, such as increases in productivity, elimination of operator errors and reduced labour needs for higher output. Up to the present time these machines have been mainly suitable for large production runs of particular components but advances in design are enabling them to be used for much reduced volumes of any one component.

However, as one would expect, the capital costs of starting a facility based on this technology are substantial! I anticipate between £50,000 and £100,000. It is for this reason that I am unable to start my sub-contract facility with machines of this calibre. Bearing this in mind I intend to start my facility with the best second-hand machines that I can get for the capital I have. I propose to start by buying two basic machine tools, namely a centre lathe and a vertical borer plus auxiliary machines such as tool and drill grinders costing about £10,000 in total. [An example of this innovation is attached as Appendix 1.1.] These machines will enable me to obtain sub-contract work from various engineering companies in the light to medium range. To give myself a competitive edge I am considering the possibility of adding suitable automation processes to these machines such as now exist on the market. [I anticipate my total start-up costs to be around £20,000.] Updating of basic machine tools looks feasible when compared with the outlay required for purpose built machines of the type mentioned previously. It is my intention, once ' established, to move into com-pletely automated machines wherever possible, as the growth of my company allows.

The market I am particularly interested in sub-contracting to is the aerospace industry, for example, Rolls Royce. This market appears to me to give the most opportunity for growth over the next decade. Providing I can obtain suitable premises in my own area of Bath, I shall in the first instance approach my previous employer and a number of other firms in the area for work. By establishing myself in this way it will enable me to approach firms such as Rolls Royce, hopefully having gained a reputation for quality work, good delivery times and price.

If it proves impossible for me to obtain premises in my local area I shall look at the possibility of moving to a development area elsewhere in the British Isles, though I would need to investigate each proposal carefully to ensure that I would not become isolated from potential customers.

I shall not be employing anyone at the outset of my business though I hope to employ someone on a part-time basis from December in the first year to enable me to keep up machining time whilst acquiring further business.

I cannot stress strongly enough my belief that the use of the new generation of high technology machine tools represents the best opportunity for the engineering industry in this country to recapture its home market, from which it will once again be able to compete successfully in the world market. We simply must get back to making things competitively, rather than acting as a consumer to the rest of the world. In my own case, by using this new technology, I intend to establish a 'centre of excellence' in machining.

DISCUSSION POINTS

Case A – This case should start the discussion of the skills and goals necessary to start a business. In particular:
  – What skills does Alan Sealey appear to have?
  – How realistic is he about the market?
  – What problems might he face in realising his dream?

Appendix 1.1: Extract from *The Financial Times* 7 March 1978

TALISMAN describes equipment by Toolmasters Controls for automating basic machine tools – lathes, drills and mills – in a most simple and inexpensive way. The technology has been kept unsophisticated, and it can be adapted to fit either new or existing equipment.

Both single and multiple work-pieces can be produced. In the case of multiples, as the operator makes the first piece, all the movements of the machine are recorded on a magnetic tape cassette. When played back, this will reproduce exactly all the machine movements, without the inevitable delays which result if drawings or charts have to be interpreted.

Talisman can control not only the basic machine movements but also the spindle, coolant, clamps, copy slides, rotary indexing table, indexing tool posts – in all, up to eight auxiliary functions can be controlled.

Individual display modules show the position of each machine axis, and control its movements.

Each module has two interdependent counters which indicate either the position from an absolute datum point or an incremental movement. Push-buttons, marked with simple arrows, cause the machine to move. The feed-rate of the machine movement is selected by a rotary switch on the display, to give rapid, jog, or controlled feed-rate. The machine moves on a predetermined distance when the required figure is dialled on the thumbwheel switches and the direction button is pressed.

The display modules generate pulses which are fed by way of the cassette recording unit to the motor drives; these provide the power for the stepping motors and drive the screws relating to each machine axis. The cassette recorder registers the pulse trains and also the signals for the auxiliary functions and, on play-back, takes complete control of the machine tool.

Toolmasters Controls, Perimeter Road, Woodley, Reading, Berks RG5 4SX.

Appendix 1.2: Letter from the *Guardian*

THE GUARDIAN

119 FARRINGDON ROAD
LONDON EC1R 3ER

Telephone 01-278 2332
Telex 8811746/7/8 (GUARDN G)
Registered in England No. 908396

Registered Office 164 Deansgate
Manchester M60 2RR
061-832 7200
Telex 667871 (manguardian mcr.)

28 March

Dear Mr Sealey,

I don't know whether you will have seen this in the Guardian on Saturday. I hope you will forgive me for giving you a new name and deliberately fudging some of the personal details you gave me - I had promised not to quote you. And I hope, too, that you will feel it gives a broadly accurate picture of the conversation. As you can see, I certainly found it interesting!

Yours sincerely,

Frances Cairncross

A.D.Sealey Esq.,
Bath.

Appendix 1.3: Article in the *Guardian*, Saturday March 25 1978

Questions and answers

The most interesting half hour I have spent in the past few days has been on the phone to a young man whom I'll call Peter. Peter is a 24-year-old turner with a medium-sized engineering firm in the West Midlands.

I rang him because he had written to the newspapers, complaining that while everyone thought that British firms did not invest enough, the real problem was that when they did invest, they made bad buys and used their new machinery inefficiently.

That seemed to me extremely plausible, and I wanted to know how he had reached such a conclusion. After half an hour on the phone, I felt I understood a great deal more about that hoary old question, what's wrong with British industry. But I also felt perversely optimistic.

The conversation went roughly like this:

Peter: What I was thinking of when I wrote was a new machine tool our firm has just bought. It cost about £80,000. It's a central lathe-turner, and they bought it to replace an old machine which has been doing the job for 20 years, but is pretty-well worn out.

When the new machine arrived, it turned out it was slower than the old one. At first, the management blamed us, and said it was low productivity. But then they complained to the firm that sold them the machine.

That firm sent a man down to look at it, and he told them it was never intended to do the job they were using it for.

Me: How on earth did they buy it in the first place?

Peter: Well, this is the thing. They sent some chaps up to look at it before they bought it, but they were all from the management – the plant engineer and the planning engineer and so on.

There were none of the operators who were actually going to use it. They would have been able to see the snags.

We have a committee which talks about new machines, but only after they have been ordered. Now of course the management have admitted they bought the wrong machine.

Me: Perhaps part of the problem is the kind of people who go into middle management. In some firms the typical works manager seems to be an older chap who wants steady hours and who doesn't have any particular management talent.

Peter: The trouble in our firm is that the people who get promoted from the shop floor are never the ones with high productivity. They'd rather anyone who was productive stayed on a machine. Of course, a lot of them don't mind, because if you get promoted to the planning office you earn less money at first. But the younger chaps do want to get into planning office jobs because they see it as a stepping stone to promotion.

Me: How did you come into engineering?

Peter: I did my four years' apprenticeship here. Then I did a year in the merchant navy. I've been back here for four years now.

Me: Why do you think that more school-leavers don't want to go into engineering?

Peter: I don't think the firms take enough trouble about their image. Engineering can be the most exciting thing in the world. But the firms never try to tell people that. Take my firm. At the moment, it's making a new kind of floating dock which is going to replace the ordinary dry dock for ships.

It's a marvellous thing – really marvellous. But nobody on the shop-floor has any idea what it looks like.

They said they'd try to get us a photo, but they haven't done so yet.

The other thing is that they don't look after the apprentices enough. There isn't enough supervision – and then they complain that the apprentices finish their four years and don't know enough. Part of the trouble is that the supervisor has been stuck in the same job since I was doing my apprenticeship, and he's given up caring.

It's the same thing in the planning office. A lot of people get into the planning office and get stuck there. Sometimes I feel that the only way to get further is to leave the firm.

Me: What about the money? Do you think that has an influence on why people go into engineering?

Peter: It must do. Why, round here bus drivers and bakers earn more than skilled engineering workers. I'm on the night shift now, but the only reason is that it's better money. If I was working days I would only be getting £65 to £67 for 40 hours.

Me: What about the unions?

Peter: That's part of the trouble. We've got the TGWU and the AEU in here, and the TGWU is easily the biggest. Most people belong to it because it costs less. But of course, there are a lot of semi-skilled and even unskilled men in it. Most of the shop stewards are semi-skilled men – perhaps because most of the skilled men are either in their fifties and sixties, or else under thirty.

The shop stewards can hardly go into negotiations and say they want a lot more money for some of their men than for others, can they?

The result is that you get semi-skilled men earning the same hourly rate as skilled men. And some of them are starting to use the same machines as skilled men, which I don't think is right. The differentials have got a lot worse in the last two years, of course, with the pay policy.

Me: Has the firm been losing skilled men?

Peter: Oh yes. About eight skilled men have left from my bit of the firm in the past year, and some have gone out of engineering altogether. The thing I really can't understand is that the firm doesn't seem to mind. I suppose work is a bit slack now, but I don't know how they would manage if it picked up suddenly.

A friend of mine left just last week. He was one of the best turners my age. He went to work for another engineering firm in Bristol. The firm didn't try to beg him to stay, of anything. They just let him go.

I know that managers have got problems – that they feel they don't have enough incentives and so on. But I wish they would try and make people feel they mattered a bit more.

PETER is not, as far as I could gather in half an hour, an agitator or a professional grumbler. He didn't volunteer the name of his firm. His main feeling about his union was resentment that it hadn't even bothered to negotiate a proper pension scheme.

He seemed to me to be sensible, ambitious and perceptive. I hope he will be running a medium-sized engineering firm in 20 years' time.

If he is, and if there are a few others like him, then feeling optimistic about British engineering will not be simply perverse.

FRANCES CAIRNCROSS

Case B*

1 Seamach

Alan Sealey confronted a classical start-up obstacle when establishing Seamach Engineering. The Bank had agreed to endorse a loan designed to help finance Seamach's start-up, contingent upon Alan securing orders from customers. Potential customers agreed to give Alan subcontract work only after he obtained the proper equipment. A contact Alan met whilst on the New Enterprise Programme at London Business School solved his dilemma. Pete, a 50 per cent owner in Robin Engineering [Robin Engineering sales in 1979 exceeded £1 million] offered to give Seamach its first subcontract machining work. He also offered to Alan a drill press, small machining equipment and a barn in which to set up the machining operations. Alan had already purchased a milling machine and a lathe for £5,000. The intervention of Robin Engineering enabled Seamach to begin operations.

Based on the arrangements made with Robin, Alan secured a £5,000 bank overdraft. Since Seamach was able to lease equipment from Robin the initially requested loan was no longer needed. To be competitively priced Alan charged the going rate of £6 per hour for his machining subcontract work. To ensure profitability his one-man operation relied on increased turnover rates. In the day he worked on machining and at night he kept Seamach's account books. During the first six months of operations Seamach Engineering turned over £7,500 worth of business, close to 90 per cent of the subcontract work coming from Robin Engineering.

2 The Proposition

Robin Engineering was started in 1974 by the two Petes as equal partners. By 1980 it acted as a holding company for seven firms concentrated in machine tooling and sheet metal fabrication. In October 1980 they approached Alan with an offer to purchase Seamach Engineering. Alan would become a director and a 5 per cent shareholder in Weltofit, a recently acquired addition to Robin Engineering. In exchange, Robin would take over Seamach's £1,400 bank overdraft and all of the assets.

Alan was tempted. Seamach was not growing as fast as he had hoped and did not have the future he had originally invisaged. Robin's proposal provided him with an opportunity to get out of Seamach

*This case was written by Rick Remick and Margie Ward.

without losing his £5,000 investment. If he liquidated the company he felt he would only get around £2,500 for the machines. Alternatively, if Robin acquired Seamach, Alan's investments in the machines would be protected.

DISCUSSION POINTS

Case B —   — What, if anything, has gone wrong?
         — Should it have been forecast?
         — Should Alan accept the offer from Robin Engineering?

2 THE CHOICE OF PARTNERS: LIGHT ENGINEERING*

> I really think that we could do better on our own – at least,
> we would have the freedom to develop the business our way.
> But how do we decide?

Alan Reed was talking to his colleagues Fred Dean and Mike Schofield. The three made up the entire board and management team of a very tiny subsidiary of a larger subsidiary of a very large manufacturing conglomerate. Their company had been acquired in 1978 and since then their own division had been neglected. Since they had all been closely involved in the initial technological development and subsequent marketing of their product they felt very frustrated by the new parent companies lack of commercial exploitation of it.

Fred Dean If this product was given the right backing, it could form the basis of a very profitable business. Instead, we are so starved of resources that we are showing constant losses and are in danger of losing any competitive advantage we might have had.

Mike Schofield I agree that we could probably start up on our own with very little money. After all, the designs are all in our heads and it isn't as though they are patentable. I am sure that the customers stay because of us and in spite of the treatment they get. I'll bet that at least half would come with us and that would mean guaranteed sales of at least £150,000 in our first year.

Alan Reed My only worry is whether there is potential growth beyond our current sales of £250,000. They do represent the total market and they have been hard to land. Although those customers are now convinced, and although there are thousands of potential uses for the system, I wonder how long it would take any others to take us seriously.

Fred Dean Don't you worry. I reckon that I could convert at least a couple of leads into orders. After all, there is no doubt that it is a

*This case was written by Sue Birley.

superb system – why else would it have been demonstrated on 'Tomorrow's World'.*

Alan Reed Yes but that was five years ago and no other company has entered the market.

Fred Dean That is because they didn't know how to use it. Now that we have done the development work and found some uses, I am sure that it is only a matter of time.

Fred Dean (57) was the oldest of the three potential partners and responsible for marketing. He was a very forceful character, disliked by the other two on a personal level but respected for his experience and selling skills. The contacts that he had built up over many years meant that he could engineer an entry into a large number of organisations. Once in, he was difficult to dislodge. He viewed the other two as 'necessary technicians'.

Alan Reed (36) was the product manager, responsible partly for design but mainly for managing the transition from drawing board, through production to installation in the clients premises. He was the person, rather than Fred, who customers turned to when difficulties arose. He preferred to spend his time in design work. Indeed his skills in this area were not inconsiderable. But he recognised that neither of the other two were in the slightest bit interested in the manufacturing process. Whilst such an attitude was understandable in Fred, he found it irritating in Mike. However, his modest personality had led him to conclude that Mike's design skills were better than his own.

Mike Schofield (26) had graduated only two years previously with a doctorate in engineering. He was fascinated by the opportunity to spend his time in design work and so was prepared to tolerate Fred's 'overbearing personality' and Alan's 'pedestrian thinking'.

DISCUSSION POINTS

This case should expand the discussion of the entrepreneur to include the question of partners. In particular, it should set up the later discussion of Steel Fabricators Ltd.

    – What can be inferred about the skills and goals of the three

*A television programme about new technological breakthrough.

partners?
- Are these either sufficient or compatible?
- What problems could they face when leaving their current employment?

3 THE DEAL BETWEEN PARTNERS: THE BOX*

While travelling on business in the USA, John Cambiare noticed a storage system which appeared to have a significant demand in a segment of a market which had not been developed in Europe. He sought out the manufacturers who were a small family company and started to negotiate for the distribution rights in Europe.

On returning to the UK he approached John Pyke and asked him if he would be interested in starting a company supplying product and services to a particular market.

John Pyke's background was in industrial marketing. He had started as a salesman in the electronic components industry and had developed to a position where he had been responsible for many new product launches and national negotiations. He had an MSc in marketing and was currently marketing manager of the division of a major multinational company.

While John Cambiare was also involved in marketing it was at corporate level where he controlled the international co-ordination of product development and promotion. He was an Italian based in the UK who had an American MBA. His position allowed him to travel throughout the western hemisphere with a concentration of activity in Europe.

The two had first met when they worked for the same organisation. Cambiare had been responsible for product development in the UK. They both were aware of each other's achievements and abilities and had kept in touch after their career paths diverged.

At first the product, which was a portable storage system for computer tapes, did not appear to have a particularly large potential market as far as Pyke was concerned. However, on researching the market he discovered that not only was the market both large and potentially profitable but also the product was the ideal launch into the untapped European segment of the market.

The capital required to start up the business would be supplied by Cambiare who had allocated £40,000 – a greater sum than was needed. Pyke was to be appointed Managing Director of the newly formed company and would receive a basic salary slightly less than his current

*This case was written by John Flyn.

one. He would, however, also receive one-third of the profit with half of the remainder going to Cambiare. Equity in the company would be divided 25 per cent to John Pyke and 75 per cent to John Cambiare. Initially Cambiare would be a non-executive director who would be funding the operation and during business trips researching the market. In addition, he would be assisting in questions of import and export and locating and investigating new products. Pyke would launch the company, establish a UK base, and develop the home market. They would jointly launch into new markets once the company had become established and could support them both.

The venture was seen as a chance for them to start their own company and break away from the restraints of a business career. Pyke had the opportunity to start without the financial risk while Cambiare could launch a company without initially putting his career in jeopardy. In both cases it seemed the ideal situation.

DISCUSSION POINTS

The deal set up between John Cambiare and John Pyke appeared to be ideal.

- What is its success likely to be based upon?
- As John Pyke, you decide that it is unacceptable, decide a new deal to be negotiated.

4 EVALUATING THE BUSINESS PLAN: CONTINENTAL TRUCKING LTD*

CONTINENTAL TRUCKING LIMITED

55 Gloucester Road,
LONDON   SW7

2nd June, 1977

ICFC,
LONDON.

Dear Sir,

This report tries to show exactly how a European haulage
company called Continental Trucking Limited could be set
up and managed by myself in Dover, England. The initial
capital needed is £107,000 and I possess £10,000 which I
would be more than willing to invest. I previously
managed Storesafe Limited a transport company in Hudders-
field, Yorkshire, for two years during which time it was
profitable returning 22% before interest and tax on fixed
assets.

If you are interested in further discussions based upon
the report please contact me at the above address.

Yours faithfully,

R. K. Brown

Introduction

European haulage is normally approached as a 'hand to mouth' business, i.e. most hauliers take the first load they can find at the beginning of the week. This is primarily because of the structure of the industry. Seventy-eight per cent of all traffic carried is by haulage companies of three or less vehicles, the vast majority of these companies being run by an owner driver or ex-driver. Though sophisticated in their driving

*This case was prepared by Richard Brown.

techniques and vehicle technology, their approach to marketing, financial planning and control, corporate strategy and profit maximisation is not so much amateurish as generally non-existent. This explains the low average returns normally associated with the road haulage industry.

This report is divided into five sections and outlines the corporate strategy I would pursue to create a profitable company:

1. A brief statement of the company structure.
2. Identification of the most profitable markets.
3. Marketing strategy.
4. Budgets for the first twelve months trading.
5. Future development of the company.

1. Continental Trucking Ltd (CTL)

CTL would be located in Dover providing a general haulage service concentrating on the European market, making CTL a net exporter. It would consist of:

FIXED ASSETS	PURCHASE PRICE
	(£)
1 Portokabin	4,000
Office Furniture	2,000
1 Car	2,500
3 DAF Tractor Units	51,000
5 Tilt Semi-Trailers	27,500
Total	87,000

Only a small site would be necessary to accommodate the portokabin and vehicles as the vehicles would be abroad most of the time with a maximum of one tractor unit and three trailers parked up at any one time. There are many sites such as these in Dover situated outside the docks.

Personnel

I would work in the company full time as General Manager, employing an assistant, and three drivers. My job would be dealing with all the administration, i.e. book-keeping, invoicing, wages and management control accounts, as well as scheduling the wagons and making all strategic decisions. The assistant's job would be selling trailer space directly to industrial customers.

Maintenance

This would be subcontracted out to the local DAF dealer. The wagons carry a twelve-month unlimited mileage guarantee.

2. Identification of the Most Profitable Markets

Problems arise in reaching worthwhile comparative data because of the following which combine to create 'lost' days. These lost days have to be accounted for in any calculations.

(i) Regulations on drivers' hours: a driver is only allowed to drive for a maximum of eight hours a day and 48 hours in any seven consecutive days – i.e. one rest day a week.
(ii) Continental regulations: it is forbidden to drive a goods vehicle (unless it contains perishables) in many European countries on Sundays. Obviously the rest day and Sundays should coincide.
(iii) The driver will need time off between each trip.
(iv) Routine maintenance is needed once a week. Again servicing takes place on days' off.

Therefore to obtain maximum utilisation a driver would have to drive for six days a week, reaching home on Saturday night and servicing would have to take place on his day off, the Sunday.

In addition maximum profitability is not a result of maximum utilisation, as other factors have to be taken into the equation. However, since overheads are fixed, contribution rather than profitability can be analysed.

To calculate the contribution, the variables are as listed below.

Price

For a given round trip the higher the price the higher the contribution.

Cost of Ferries

These vary according to which channel-crossing route is used, the length of the vehicle train and in some cases, such as dangerous goods, the goods carried. They also depend very much on the shipping agents as most of them give discounts which vary in magnitude according to amount of traffic and company creditworthiness. Most of the shipping agents are entrepreneurs with a portokabin, a telex and an account with a shipping line. The agent acts for various haulage companies and by putting their combined traffic through on his account he obtains a large discount from the shipping line. A smaller discount is passed on to each haulier but this discount is higher than that which they could obtain individually.

Expenses

These can consist of:

(a) Road tolls – payable in most but not all European countries, on motorway-type roads and tunnels, e.g. Mont Blanc.

(b) 'Night-out money' – this is defined by the Ministry of Transport as subsistence payments to compensate the drivers for the extra cost of living away from home. In reality these payments are used as a means of providing the driver with extra remuneration, particularly as they are free of tax.

(c) Telephone or telex costs – incurred when a driver reports either his position or a new development.

(d) Fines – for speeding or contravening a European country's legislation. For example it is illegal to enter certain countries with more than a few gallons of diesel in the tractor unit tanks but with only these few gallons it is impossible to reach a service station. In this situation the only practical solution is to carry a large amount of diesel and pay the fine if caught.

(e) Bribe money – usually used to minimise or eliminate fines.

Opportunity Cost of 'Lost Days'

This is equal to the amount of contribution that could be earned if the driver and unit were being used on another job. This is impossible to quantify because there is no standard job and there is no guarantee that work would be available on that particular load. It is possible, however, to quantify the direct standing costs, i.e. salary and 'night-out money'. This cost is £18.50 per day.

Running Costs Per Mile

These are represented by:

Diesel	12p
Tyre wear	3.5p
Maintenance	3.5p

Driver bonus   1p
Total running cost per mile   20p

From this, a basic contribution model can be constructed:

Contribution = Total price − (ferry cost + expenses + opportunity cost)
− (running cost per mile x number of miles run)

This model is useful in three forms.

(a) Total Contribution Per Year. This assumes that it is possible to obtain traffic to and from a specific area on a regular basis. It is rare that one can get much regular traffic but it is a very useful model, if looked at 'backwards', for comparing which are the most profitable markets when obtaining regular traffic. This can deliberately concentrate the company's marketing resources to generate sufficient traffic. The ideal position is to have surplus capacity which can be sub-contracted out to other haulers and owner drivers. Generally the most profitable haulage companies deal directly with the company whose goods they are carrying. However, these are in the minority, the vast majority depend upon subcontracted work, at a reduced rate.

A standard year is 44 working weeks − the other eight are taken up by major overhauls on the wagons and on holidays.

(b) Contribution Per Trip. This is useful for comparing one trip against another when one can only plan in the short term. Most useful with trips of the same or similar duration.

(c) Contribution Per Day. This is most useful for comparing trips of different duration. Other factors must also be considered such as availability for new work upon completion of the trip.

Form (a) is the best for establishing the most profitable target markets.
The results of comparability are shown in Table 4.1. Obviously the most profitable market to concentrate on is France.

3. Marketing Strategy

Haulage is a very competitive market with many suppliers and purchasers, and demand is directly dependent upon the amount of general economic activity. The hauliers who are in direct contact with companies needing haulage receive the highest prices. These hauliers are in the minority and subcontract out their excess capacity to other hauliers, having taken a commission. In the main, prices are set by the market but there are times when a premium can be charged. These are:

(a) When carrying valuable loads. The transport costs are a small percentage of the total value and so not as sensitive to variences.
(b) When carrying perishables.
(c) When making 'express' deliveries.

The CTL salesman will concentrate on these three areas, utilising the many contacts he already has in the industry. It is crucial that any customers obtained are given first-class service, especially for express deliveries, as haulage is a repeat order business. Advertising would be confined to personal gifts such as desk diaries, given out by the salesman when he calls. Building up a name for reliability, which is a great barrier to entry, can be achieved in six months, but it can be lost overnight.

Table 4.1: Comparability Results

Country	Contribution/Trip	No. of trips	Total contribution/std year/wagon
France	£350	73.3	£25,670
Italy	£400	44	£17,600
Belgium	£210	73.3	£15,400

4. Future Development of the Company

Apart from the obvious development of expansion of the haulage fleet should there be a demand, related fields should also be considered.

(a) Clearing Agent

Customs clearance work which can be done with no increase in fixed assets. Extra personnel would be needed and the company must be more than one year old before a bank guarantee, which will satisfy customs and excise, can be obtained. The return on the incremental cost is very high.

(b) 'T' Form Agent

Making out Community Transit Forms for hauliers on their outward journey to Europe. These forms allow the haulier to pass across international borders without his paying duty on the goods. Again this needs a bank guarantee for customs and excise so the company must be one year old. This carries a higher risk than being a clearing agent the risk of default whereas clearance work requires prior payment. The returns are high.

(c) Warehousing and Distribution

This involves high financial outlay on the purchase rental of a warehouse but the risk can be reduced greatly by canvassing our existing customers prior to reaching any decision.

5. Budgets for the First Twelve Months' Trading

On the following pages there are five exhibits. These show:

Exhibit 1. Profit and loss account for the first twelve months' trading.
Exhibit 2. Balance sheet for the first twelve months' trading.
Exhibit 3. Funds flow for the first twelve months' trading.
Exhibit 4. Monthly cash flow.

Exhibits 1, 2 and 3 were built up from Table 4.1 and the theory expounded in section 3. It was assumed that in the first two months the company ran at 50 per cent standard capacity. The final figures shown in Exhibits 1, 2, 3 and 4 are *extremely* sensitive to any fluctuation in price as the fluctuation is multiplied 200 times.

Exhibit 4 shows the cash deviations due to trading but does not include the initial £20,000 capital nor the repayments of capital plus interest in June and December.

DISCUSSION POINTS

A formal proposal has been put to ICFC.
   — How does the student evaluate the layout and content of the proposal?
   — Richard Brown is proposing to enter a highly competitive market.

Is there anything unique or special about his particular business? Does he understand the elements necessary for success?

— Does this business need money and, if so, would they lend on the basis of the data available?

Exhibit 1: Profit and Loss Account for First Twelve Months of Trading

		£'000
SALES		194
COST OF GOODS SOLD:		
WAGES + NIGHT OUT MONEY	19.8	
TOLLS	4	
SEA FREIGHT	54	
RUNNING COSTS	46	123.8
	GROSS PROFIT	70.2
LESS		
OFFICE SALARIES	9	
INSURANCE	5.5	
VEHICLE TAX	3	
GROUND RENT/RATES	3	
DEPRECIATION	17.4	
TELEX & TELEPHONE	4	
MARKETING	3	
OFFICE O/H + STATIONERY	1	45.9
Profit before interest + tax		24.3

Assume 5 year loan at 10% flat rate interest on full
£87,000 - Interest = £8,700   2.79 times covered.
Return on net fixed assets before interest and tax = 34.7%
Two repayments per year to ICFC of £8,700 capital + £4,350 interest

@ 30 June and 31 December.   TOTAL £13,050

Exhibit 2: Balance Sheet at the end of First Twelve Months Trading

LIABILITIES			ASSETS	
		£'000		£'000
20,000 £1 shares		20	FIXED ASSETS	87
From P + L		15.6	LESS DEPCN	17.4
Shareholders funds		35.6		69.6
LOAN FROM ICFC	87			
LESS AMOUNT REPAID	17.4	69.6		
		105.2		
CURRENT LIABILITIES			CURRENT ASSETS	
CREDITORS		5.0	DEBTORS 14.1	
			CASH 26.5	41
		110.2		110.2

Exhibit 3: Funds Flow Statement for First Year's Trading

FUNDS FLOW STATEMENT FOR FIRST YEARS TRADING

	£'000	
SOURCE OF FUNDS		
LOAN FROM ICFC	87	
INCREASE IN SHARE CAPITAL	20	
PROFIT BEFORE INTEREST	24.3	
DEPRECIATION	17.4	148.7
LESS USES OF FUNDS		
PURCHASE OF FIXED ASSETS	87	
REPAYMENT OF LOAN	17.4	
PAYMENT OF INTEREST	8.7	113.1
		35.6
REPRESENTED BY		
INCREASE IN CREDITORS	(5)	
INCREASE IN DEBTORS	14.1	
INCREASE IN CASH	26.5	35.6
		35.6

Exhibit 4: Cash Flow Budget for First Twelve Months' Trading

	JAN	FEB	MAR	APR	MAY	JUNE	JULY	AUG	SEPT	OCT	NOV	DEC	TOTALS
RECEIPTS		3000	9700	19400	19400	19400	19400	19400	19400	19400	19400	19400	179900
LESS:													
WAGES + NIGHTS OUT	1650												19800
TOLLS	200	200	400	400	400	400	400	200	400	400	400	400	4000
SEA FREIGHT		2700	2700	5400	5400	5400	5400	5400	2700	5400	5400	5400	51200
DIRECT RUNNING COSTS		2300	2300		4600	4600	4600	4600	2300	4600	4600	4600	43700
OFFICE SALARIES)													
OFFICE O/H)													
MARKETING)	1666												20000
PHONE + TELEX)													
GROUND RENT)													
INSURANCE)	8500												8500
VEHICLE TAX)													
MONTHLY CASH FLOW	(12016)	(5516)	984	(10864)	(5180)	508	5684	5884	3284	5684	5684	5684	
CUMULATIVE CASH FLOW	(12016)	(17532)	(16548)				6188	12072	15356	21040	26724	32668	
NO OF TRIPS	10	10	20	20	20	20	20	10	20	20	20	10	

5 FITTING THE PRODUCT TO THE MARKET: LINGUA FRANCA*

Robert Barclay founded Lingua Franca to meet the demand from foreign company executives seeking to learn or improve their English by providing high quality, high intensity, residential language courses. Robert: 'Many companies and individuals are fed up with the bureaucracy involved in dealing with a large school and often appreciate the flexibility which can be offered by a smaller organisation.'

In May 1979 Robert negotiated an agreement with University College Oxford for seminar rooms and 75 bedrooms to be leased during two months in the summer of 1980. By January 1980, brochures had been printed and Robert had begun his marketing effort. However he was faced with two major problems. First, some of the potential clients he had seen were unhappy that he was only offering one-month courses and indicated that two weeks would be more attractive. Should Robert offer four two-week courses as well as two one-month courses, and at what price?

Second, Robert as owner and sole proprietor would be responsible for setting up and marketing the school and its programmes. However, he intended to employ a Principal to be responsible for the actual planning, building and co-ordination of the courses and a Director of Studies to ensure their smooth running. But what sort of people should he be looking for and how should he recognise them? After all, this would be the first time he had employed anyone.

The Courses

The first Lingua Franca programme would be held at University College Oxford, in the summer of 1980. There would be two one-month courses each catering for a maximum of 75 students, all of whom would be highly motivated and from similar job backgrounds. All tuition, meals and accommodation in private rooms would be in the college, and students would be given 30 hours' tuition a week in small

*This case was written by Sue Birley from material provided by Robert Barclay, Symon Elliott, Aneel Nanji and Stephen Stringer.

groups with a maximum of seven students in any one group. Activities of various kinds, such as discussion groups, lectures, film shows, excursions, would be organised every evening and also at week-ends so that the student would never have to feel at a loose end. The most modern teaching methods would be used to give the student an even balance of speaking and comprehension skills, though there would be no written practice. All teachers at Lingua Franca would be graduates and highly experienced in teaching English to business people. They would have to have a thorough understanding of the problems students faced when learning a new language, and would thus be equipped to deal effectively with them.

Robert felt that the success of any course largely depended on three factors: (i) the teaching staff; (ii) the students; (iii) the location.

Robert The emphasis at Lingua Franca is on commercial English, and the aim of the school is to immerse students totally in English-speaking situations.

Lingua Franca is not unique in this field but intends to make a name for itself by providing excellent service and a high level of personal attention to its students. At Lingua Franca the beginner is guaranteed the ability to communicate in English after one month, even if this necessitates removing the student from a group and providing him/her with individual tuition at no extra cost. All students will be continually supervised by the Director of Studies which will thus enable him to monitor the progress of all course participants. It is hoped that the innovative methods of grading students carefully into groups, the full schedule of social activities and the first-rate teaching staff will give Lingua Franca the reputation of 'a school with a difference'.

The most important task facing Lingua Franca is that of developing a solid reputation and goodwill. Gradual expansion is planned and this will be done by increasing places on courses by 50 per cent for 1981 and running two programmes simultaneously (one at Cambridge) in 1982. It can therefore be assumed that by the end of 1982 approximately 800 students will have attended courses at Lingua Franca. Working on this assumption, a wide enough reputation will have been established to proceed with plans to set up an exclusive English language school for executives, possibly in permanent premises, in central London in 1983/4.

The Market and the Industry

Postwar, English came to the fore as the leading business and diplomatic language. As a result, language schools began to mushroom in the early 1950s and the rapidly growing market happily carried with it all the schools which started, regardless of the quality of teaching or the commercial acumen of the owners. Three types of schools which flourished in this period are described briefly in Appendix 5.1.

In 1980 the demand for language courses could be segmented as follows:

Individuals from abroad seeking:
(1) Holiday/language courses.
(2) Part-time tuition in groups.
(3) Full-time tuition in groups.
(4) Full-time intensive courses in small groups.
(5) Part-time intensive courses in small groups.

Companies from abroad seeking:
(6) Full-time intensive courses for their employees either in groups or on a one to one basis.

Foreign individuals in England seeking:
(7) Any of the above.

There were, of course, schools catering for all these needs, though no statistics had been published so it was difficult to follow any trends in the market. However, the TEFL (teaching English as a foreign language) market was estimated to be worth around £80m, catering for about 200,000 students with 250 schools offering about 800 courses. It could loosely be divided into two main categories, each facing different environmental and competitive pressures.

1. The Leisure/Holiday Market

This was the sector which offered short courses of between three and five weeks, mainly in the summer time, to two-thirds of all students who came to Britain between June and September. Plenty of spare time was built into the courses and the students tended to be young.

In such cases, the tour operator acted as agent, buying courses wholesale from the school in England and retailing them through their own outlets in a package which also included the necessary travel arrangements. Usually their profit was made on the discount received from both the language school and the airline used.

Small UK-based operations were facing severe competition from these tour operators, especially with the strengthening of the pound, which had hit the holiday market as a whole. The top ten schools in terms of fee taking, seven of which were foreign owned, were estimated to take just over a third of the total fees, with the largest taking 15 per cent.

2. The Professional Market

This market was distinct from the leisure/holiday market in four main ways:

(i) Courses were both short and long.
(ii) Courses were held all the year round.
(iii) Courses were generally more intensive.
(iv) Most important: there was a professional purpose behind taking the course.

There were two segments within the professional market, distinguished by the nature of professional purpose behind taking the course:

(a) Qualification Participants took exams for University or school entrance requirements abroad, generally culminating in taking Cambridge Certificate, GCE or other recognised proficiency exams. Students were usually relatively young and large leisure/holiday companies had found it quite easy to expand into this market to fill capacity throughout the year.

(b) Vocational Courses oriented towards business interests or employment. As well as businessmen this group could include TEFL teachers; professionals such as doctors, lawyers, engineers or the clergy; administrators from local government. Generally participants were older than for the previous segment. Courses were short and intensive with participants usually sponsored by their organisations.

Supply was highly fragmented, with many small, specialised schools. Only a few companies offered a range of specialist courses with a core of adaptable teachers.

In 1980 the qualification market was experiencing a similar concentration to the leisure/holiday sector, mainly because the large schools referred to above were filling capacity during the rest of the year from this segment. The size of the market appeared to be plateauing, not being as sensitive as the holiday markets to the strength of the pound.

The vocational market appeared to offer most hope to the small business man since there was an unlimited range of specialist course which could be offered and the costs of entry needed not to be very high.

The British Tourist Authority estimated that there would be 800 courses of various kinds running in the summer of 1980, though this figure was unhelpful due to the many different kinds of courses on offer. Robert felt, however, that the boom enjoyed by schools in the people coming from abroad had suffered at a lower level. Despite the fact that many schools had suffered from this decline, those at the lower end of the market selling courses at a low price to young people and those dealing exclusively with companies appeared to have maintained some equilibrium. Although there appeared to be no real data on the market for teaching English, an article in the *Sunday Times* did throw light on some of the difficulties of learning a foreign language in England (see Appendix 5.2).

Premises

Premises were used by schools to varying degrees for accommodation, teaching and general administration. Most, except the very large schools, tried to avoid direct provision of accommodation, preferring either to keep in touch with local families prepared to offer student accommodation or to hire bedrooms in a local hotel. A number of the smaller schools hired space in universities during the summer which provided both accommodation as well as teaching facilities in a credible educational environment. The larger schools, particularly those offering courses the year round, found it necessary to have permanent teaching premises to provide both administrative support for the student as well as the sophisticated language laboratories not usually available in hired conference centres.

The Marketing Strategy

1. Price

The price of a one-month Lingua Franca course would be £560 (+VAT) which included tuition, accommodation, breakfast and lunch. The price would be increased by 10 per cent to £615 as of 1 February 1980. Although other schools may charge up to 25 per cent more for similar courses, Robert thought it best to keep prices down for the first year and attract students by offering a special introductory price.

2. Promotion

No direct advertising was planned, but Lingua Franca would be receiving free promotion in the form of small articles in the following publications: *Le Figaro* (France), *Der Spiegel* (Germany), *International Herald Tribune*, *Corriere Della Sere* (Italy), *Il Giornale* (Italy). In addition to this, Robert Barclay had talked about Lingua Franca in a short interview for TVI, a Milan-based television channel.

3. Sales

The majority of Lingua Franca courses would be sold direct to companies through personal visits by Robert Barclay. He had already visited 35 companies in France, Germany and Italy in December 1979 and had had a favourable reception. However, all had indicated that it was unlikely that they would make any firm bookings before May 1980. Lingua Franca courses would be marketed primarily in these countries and Robert would return to Europe in February to visit a further 200 new companies.

Lingua Franca courses would also be sold through agents in France and Italy on a commission basis, and Robert expected that these agents would send 10 per cent of the total number of students attending a course.

A direct-mail shot to companies had been considered, though after an unsuccessful trial run of 100 this idea had been dropped. However, many institutes and organisations promoting language courses had been contacted with some positive results.

The Proprietor

Robert Barclay: 'I left school in 1975 and spent the next year retaking some exams and travelling around Europe. I decided to take up accountancy in September 1976 but by December of that year I had come to the conclusion that the whole thing was a dead loss. I then took up full-time employment as an English Language teacher until August 1977 when I left England to spend 16 months travelling round India and the far East. Six months of that was spent in Japan working as a course co-ordinator for a very small English Language School. I returned to England in November 1978 and resumed work as a language teacher. In February 1979 I worked as an assistant for a Member of Parliament for four months after which I started full time work on Lingua Franca.'

Finance

Shown in Appendices 5.3-5.6 are the following:

(1) Opening balance sheet.
(2) Balance sheet at end of year one.
(3) First year profit and loss analysis.
(4) Break-even analysis.
(5) First year cash flow analysis.

Robert had already invested £3,000 of his own money in the venture and anticipated that he would need overdraft facilities for a further £5,000 in January which he saw no difficulty in obtaining.

Appendix 5.1: Three Types of Start-ups

The 'Professional' Start-up – e.g. Bell School

Founded as a charitable trust in 1955 by Frank Bell who was on the Extra-mural Board of one of the Cambridge colleges, and as such experienced in setting up new courses and looking out for new opportunities in education. He began with a capacity of 200 students in a large building in pleasant grounds in Cambridge, and employed the latest techniques in language teaching from the very start. In 1980 the Bell Group had a capacity of 720 students and was regarded as one of the most professionally run schools in the UK.

The 'Shoestring' Start-up

Started in 1972 after the owner had been fired from another TEFL school. Apart from his own £50, he was fortunate to be left £200 by a 'business partner' who subsequently had a nervous breakdown for unrelated reasons. He recruited students by 'picking them off the streets' and charging them an incredibly low £6 a week. Through a series of lucky breaks, he managed to get more students and develop a continuing relationship with the Saudi Arabian cultural attaché. In 1980, although experiencing some difficulty in the slack winter months, he had about 200 students, a freehold building and a saleable business. He planned to retire in a few years by selling the business.

The 'Dealer'

The dealer acts as an agent by renting suitable premises, recruiting students and teachers, putting them together and forming a temporary school. At the end of the course, he pays everyone off and takes what is left. The dealer is crucial in putting the many elements of the operation together and as such it is almost impossible to set up a saleable business. The returns are purely in the form of income and not capital.

Appendix 5.2: Extract from the *Sunday Times* Colour Supplement, 24 February 1980: 'Where To Learn A Language'

Adult Education Courses

The big advantage of state adult education is its cheapness and availability. Most people are within reach of a college or polytechnic offering tuition in at least the basic European languages. The cost of a year's course, of 35 two-hour evening classes, will not normally exceed £8 and may be less. Many colleges also run daytime, lunchtime and rush-hour classes, while a number offer courses in conjunction with the BBC's multi-media tuition. Class social life is an important consideration for many people.

The main disadvantage is the size of the classes. The Inner London Education Authority, for instance, demands a minimum of 9-13 students per course, too large a number for effective language teaching to a group of unselected adults. To make matters worse, colleges invariably enrol more than the stipulated minimum because of the high drop-out rate, which is notoriously high for modern languages. Another drawback is the use of teachers without formal qualifications, whose teaching methods may vary from reactionary to ultra-conservative.

Although some colleges now offer intensive courses, adult education in general should not be seen as a quick means of language acquisition.

Private Schools

Are you willing to spend between £500 and £1,000 on learning the rudiments of a foreign language? If the answer is no, you can discount individual tuition at a private school. Most estimate 120 hours as the minimum for moderate competence in French or German, and the going hourly rate is between £4.50 and £7.50.

The schools' courses are mostly geared to the needs of big business and accompanied by such high-powered tags as 'intensive' and 'total impact'. The idea of fluency within weeks is alluring, although John Trim, Director of the Centre for Information on Language Teaching and Research, warns: 'There's a tendency in industrial circles to underestimate the difficulties of language learning.'

If your firm allows you to choose between schools, analyse their teaching methods and assess their willingness to create a course for your needs. While examining their brochures, note their use of English. Can you happily entrust your tuition to people who talk in terms of 'wholly direct, programmed structure-learning courses'?

Home Study

Established home study systems cost far less than private tuition and the main advantage is that you decide when and for how long you study. It may sound tempting, but to succeed in learning a language alone requires a great deal of motivation and reassurance. The traditional home study methods involve books and postal correction, or records, tapes and cassettes. The leaders in the latter field are Linguaphone, whose courses currently cost £72.50.

Any attempt to study a language at home will be a challenge, and the more it relies on the spoken word, the less your chances of proficiency. Learning by 'Teach Yourself' books without any other assistance is not recommended.

BBC Multi-media Courses

According to John Trim, these are 'ahead of anything else in the world at this time'. Currently available in French, German, Spanish and Italian, the courses exploit every readily available learning aid: television, radio, records, cassettes, books, back-up adult education classes and postal tuition. The first-year course involves 25 TV programmes and 20-25 radio programmes together with records and cassettes which can be used at the student's convenience, and back-up classes organised at between 250 and 300 further education colleges. There is also a correspondence course with the National Extension College in Cambridge.

The link between all these elements is the written course material contained in one, two or three books on general sale at between £2 and £3 each. The popularity of the multi-media system is such that the course books have figured in the best-seller lists.

The one drawback is the lack of broadcasting time. Only two TV slots a week are available so only one new course and one repeat can be screened each year, and radio alone carries the second and third programmes. The compromise solution proposed by the BBC is a self-study kit which costs around £45 per language.

Private Tutors

Tutors can be found through local newspaper advertisements or personal recommendation, but checking your would-be mentor's knowledge qualifications is essential before committing yourself. As for learning from a friend or relative, hesitate: you may lose a friend and achieve very little.

Alternative Education

Co-operatives, workshops and study groups may be operating in your area and must be evaluated on individual merits. One example is Intercoop in Covent Garden, a teachers' co-operative where all administrative and tutorial duties are shared, which reduces administrative overheads. An eight-week course – two evenings a week in a group of not more than twelve – costs £26. Teacher Dick Cervantes describes the Co-op's stance as 'slightly left-wing' and says the content of the lessons 'may be concerned with social and political issues'.

Of course, the opportunities for improving your linguistic ability do not end with formal courses. Remember that exposure to the language in an everyday context, however mundane, is invaluable. Even the Italian pizzeria down the road has its place. Possibilities include: language clubs and societies; cultural centres, colleges and universities; trade union links; foreign newspapers and magazines; foreign radio stations; churches and émigré groups; delicatessen and food shops.

Any time spent abroad is naturally a bonus. Apart from increasing fluency and confidence, even the shortest visit will do wonders for motivation. Investigate weekend trips; they may cost much less than you think.

Appendix 5.3

1. OPENING BALANCE SHEET

Loan a/c	3,800	Fixed assets	–
Loss to date	(4,500)	Current assets	–
	(700)	Cash	–
Overdraft	700		
	£0		£0

2. FORECAST BALANCE SHEET AT END OF YEAR ONE

Loan a/c	3,800	Fixed assets	–
Profit	19,200	Current assets	–
	23,000	Cash	£23,000
	£23,000		

Appendix 5.4: Lingua Franca Forecast Profit and Loss Analysis for First Year

£'000	100 students	120 students	150 students
Revenue	56.00	67.20	84.00
Less commission	0.56	0.67	0.84
(10% on 10% of students)			
NET REVENUE	55.44	66.53	83.16
Less:			
Variable costs			
College	25.88	31.00	38.20
Teachers	12.00	14.40	18.00
	37.88	45.40	56.20
Fixed costs	16.00	16.00	16.00
	53.88	61.40	72.20
NET PROFIT	1.56	5.13	10.96
		Plus:[a]	
		Interest	4.24
		Profits from spin offs	4.00
			19.20

Note. a. These figures have been estimated only on 150 students.

Appendix 5.5: Break-even Analysis

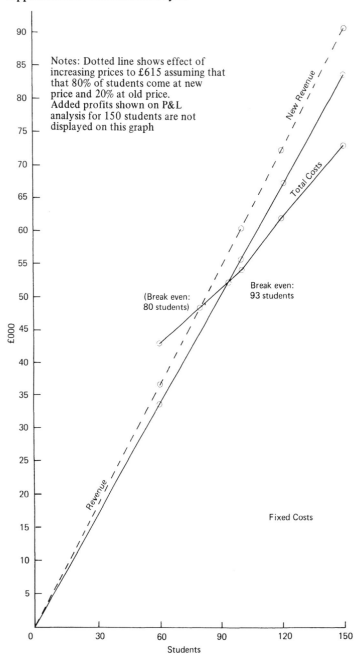

Notes: Dotted line shows effect of
increasing prices to £615 assuming that
that 80% of students come at new
price and 20% at old price.
Added profits shown on P&L
analysis for 150 students are not
displayed on this graph

New Revenue

Total Costs

(Break even:
80 students)

Break even:
93 students

Revenue

Fixed Costs

£000

Students

Appendix 5.6: Lingua Franca – Cash Flow Analysis £'000

	JAN	FEB	MAR	APR	MAY	JUN	JUL	AUG	SEP	OCT	NOV	DEC
Sales (volume)[a]												
(Full fees – £560)	20	20	30	6	4	8	5	5				
(Deposits – £129)	20	20	30	14	6	2	36	36				
(Balance – £431)												
Sales (£)		15.85	23.77	5.94	3.47	5.45	25.06[b]	25.06				
Postage					0.07				0.07			
Printing									0.5			
Telephone	0.25			0.1			0.1					
Office equipment									0.25	0.05		
Teaching aids									1.0			
Prof. services						0.5			0.25			
Course entertainment							0.5	0.5				
Wages						1.0	11.05	11.05				
Travel	1.0		0.6									
Advertising				0.25	1.0							
Insurance												
Car							0.5	0.5	2.0		0.36[e]	
VAT					4.75[c]			1.94	0.84			
Spin-offs									38.9			
Agents commission												
University college	3.4							2.0				
Less expenses	4.65	–	0.6	0.35	5.82	1.5	12.15	15.99	43.81	0.05	0.36	–
Opening balance	(0.7)[f]	(5.43)	10.57	34.13	40.18	38.27	42.71	56.27	66.10	22.55	22.76	22.66
New flow	(5.35)	10.45	33.74	39.72	37.83	42.22	55.62	65.34	22.29	22.50	22.40	22.66
Interest/loans[d]	(0.08)	0.12	0.39	0.46	0.44	0.49	0.65	0.76	0.26	0.26	0.26	0.26
Closing balance	(5.43)	10.57	34.13	40.18	38.27	42.71	56.27	66.10	22.55	22.76	22.66	23.0

Notes to Appendix 5.6: a. Sales correspond to number of bookings made. b. Included in July + August figures is £4,000/month revenue from spin-offs. c. £600 VAT output on deposits to University College. d. Interest calculated on rate 14 per cent (16 per cent) 18 per cent. e. £5,130 VAT output to University College. f. Costs incurred at this date:

	(£)
Travel	900
Deposit to UC	1,600
Printing	1,500
Miscellaneous	500
Total	£4,500

(Cash flow estimated on 150 students.)

DISCUSSION POINTS

Lingua Franca is a second example of a company in a market where the barriers to entry are low and competition high.

- What are the key elements of success in this market?
- Has Robert Barclay designed a strategy which fits the elements in the market place?

6 BARRIERS TO ENTRY FOR A NEW SERVICE: GIROGIFT – THE AIRMAIL VOUCHER SERVICE*

In the summer of 1976 Rod Senior was preparing to launch his new international gift voucher in New Zealand. This case describes his activities to date and his planned future strategy.

Introduction

Mailing gifts to and from the UK through the overseas postal system not only incurs heavy expense, long delays, breakages and losses but also is accompanied by customs and excise difficulties. Overseas parcel postal charges from the UK have risen at an alarming rate over the past twelve months to the extent that fewer people can afford the pleasure. Foreign postal rates to the UK have also been increasing at similar rates.

Clearly, there is a need for British people living abroad to be able to send a gift quickly, easily and cheaply to their relatives, friends or colleagues in the UK at Christmas and on birthdays, for example. In addition there is an equivalent reciprocal need.

To fulfil these needs I am developing an International Gift Voucher Exchange Service which provides for one to purchase and air mail a gift overseas in the form of a gift voucher greetings card which is redeemable at any branch of several leading departmental chain stores in the beneficiary's country.

Market Location

The largest density of Britons living abroad is found in Australia, New Zealand, Canada, South Africa and British Forces in Germany. The export of a UK gift voucher to these target markets will form the basis of my investigations during the summer.

*This case was prepared by Rod Senior.

Market Potential

1. Short Term

The probable size of the market potential in the above countries can be established by considering Australia as an example:

(a) Just over one million people (or 10 per cent) of the total population are British but an estimated 50 per cent of these will have 'lost touch' with the UK over time.

(b) On average, each British person has potentially three close relations or contacts in the UK to whom he/she would be likely to send a Christmas or birthday gift if a simple and cheap enabling facility was provided for them.

(c) On average $A8 per person per year is spent on overseas gift parcels to the UK.

(d) Assuming that the half a million Britons are potential in Australia for UK-bound gift vouchers is ½m x A$8 = $A4 million.

(e) This figure is enhanced even further by the number of Australians living in the UK to whom gift vouchers could be sent by their homeland relatives.

Similar reasoning can be applied to the twelve million Britons living in Canada (mainly Toronto, Vancouver), the 1/3 million in New Zealand, 80,000 families in NAAFI Germany etc. who are all potential customers for UK bound Gift Vouchers. On this basis the total overseas potential is around £30 million.

It is reasonable to assume that more than half of the UK voucher recipients would reciprocate the gesture and thus the overall market potential would be at least 50 per cent higher than the overseas potential alone, i.e. around £50 million total potential for a two-way service between UK and the prime target markets overseas.

2. Long Term

In the longer term, the potential is even greater than this on the following two grounds:

(a) There is a market for UK bound gift vouchers in other countries than those mentioned above. There are large settlements of Britons, for example, in the USA, EEC, East Africa, Middle East but they are more spread out and are subsequently a more expensive market to reach. However, they will be a very real proposition in three years' time when the business will have a sound asset base.

(b) It is intended in the longer term that the service be truly international so that agencies established in overseas countries can provide not only UK Gift Vouchers but vouchers redeemable in other countries (e.g. Canada or France). In the longer term the overall market potential for International Gift Vouchers is several times that estimated for the short term and opens up countless exciting international marketing opportunities.

Exchange Control Regulations

The Reserve Banks of Australia and New Zealand and the Bank of England impose limits on the individual amounts of cash gifts remitted abroad each year of $A1,000, $NZ100 and £1,000 respectively (£300 for non-overseas sterling areas). No such restrictions exist in Canada, South Africa or Germany.

Since vouchers are treated as cash for exchange control purposes it has been necessary to gain approval from these reserve banks to operate the scheme in those countries and copies of the relevant authorities are provided (see Appendices 6.1 and 6.2).

The Operation of the Service

In the longer run my ideal objective is to operate the international marketing of a single brand 'universal' gift voucher, printed in various denominations and currencies, redeemable at leading chain stores throughout the world, and re-encashed through a central clearing system.

However, the marginal revenue which these vouchers would initially bring to the national chain stores would be negligible compared with their added administration burden and security risk. It is clear that I would need to develop a sound, reliable business with substantial turnover before I could hope to launch my own brand of voucher.

In the short term, therefore, I intend to establish closer relationships with the various national chain store groups by exporting their own brand of gift vouchers. This will enable me to build up a reputable business which would generate substantial extra profit for the stores involved and subsequently achieve a sound base from which to operate my own brand.

Up to now I have reached agreement with the following six leading British chain stores to act as an export agent for them by marketing their own brand gift vouchers in the target countries described earlier: Boots Ltd (see Appendix 6.3), EMI (see Appendix 6.4), Debenhams, Habitat, W.H. Smith and Austin Reed. Britons overseas will obviously enjoy a very wide variety of choice of gift type for their British contacts.

To enable British recipients to reciprocate I have managed to interest a leading chain store group in all of the target countries in supplying their vouchers to me from bulk stocks held at their London Buying Agency's offices. The stores concerned are: Eatons of Canada, J.C. Penney of the USA, Greatermanns of South Africa, Waltons of Australia and Whitcoulls of New Zealand.

To avoid embarrassment caused by initial teething problems (for example, fixing exchange rates, optimum ordering) with these stores I have decided to enter formal agreement this year with only one, Whitcoulls, in order that next year I can confidently contract with the other groups on the basis of proven success and a workable system.

Profitability

I aim to achieve a gross profit margin of 20 per cent made up of 10 per cent discount on purchase of the vouchers, which most stores have agreed to, and 10 per cent from a customer service charge and exchange rate variations.

Competition

At present there is no company in the world involved in international gift voucher marketing. In the absence of direct competition it is worth noting the substitute products on the market.

Parcel Postage

As already pointed out, this is very expensive and inefficient.

Cash-mail Transfer/Draft

By far the most popular way of transmitting gifts at present. It is important, however, to draw the distinction between this cold and impersonal gift and a personalised gift voucher card with a particular store and range of gifts in mind. It is this consumer preference of vouchers instead of cash which produces a £12 million annual turnover of Boots' Gift Vouchers in this country and which has led nearly every chain store, including Woolworth's and Marks and Spencer last year (and British Home Stores and Littlewoods later this year), to introduce their own brand of voucher.

Other Goods Remittance Services

There are a few companies in operation which have kept up the wartime tradition of delivering food hampers to overseas relatives whilst one company is currently operating a Christmas-tree delivery service. Of course Interflora deliver flowers world wide by the Teleflower service but there is much evidence that there is diminishing public demand for this. Neither do I not see these other companies providing much competition.

Marketing the Vouchers

Essentially, potential customers will be approached by advertising and leaflet marketing.

The UK Market for Overseas Vouchers

The most obvious captive markets are the members of overseas clubs. My investigations to date indicate indisputably that there would be a favourable response from this market sector which totals well over 150,000 people. This year, I shall be promoting New Zealand vouchers through these clubs by means of leaflet distribution and publicity in their internal newsletters. In addition, I plan to advertise in the New Zealand and Australasian newspapers and conduct a loose-leaf insert campaign in August this year.

The leaflet contains details of the foreign store, a tear-off order form and, on the reverse, an overprinted Post Office Giro slip with special provisions for signing the Bank of England declaration (see Appendices 6.5 and 6.6). A business account with National Giro thus enables customers to make payment for their order at the local post office. As the business builds up it will be possible to develop a mailing list so that leaflets can be direct mailed to customers after the first order.

The Overseas Market for UK Gift Vouchers – Summer Project

The most obvious ready-made market this year are the beneficiaries of the New Zealand vouchers sent from the UK. These people will receive a leaflet by direct mail which will enable them to reciprocate by completing the order form and mailing it, with a sterling draft in an envelope provided, to National Giro, Liverpool where it will be processed.

There are several other ways in which these overseas target markets can be approached all requiring full investigation with regard to the media, local culture and promotional expense. The programme for the summer would be on the following lines:

(i) Examine the potential market for UK Gift Vouchers in Australia, New Zealand, Canada, South Africa and NAAFI/Germany in terms of:
    (a) Geographical areas containing the densest pockets of British people, overseas clubs and companies with British offices.
    (b) The best selection of media for reaching these people.
    (c) The likely cost-effectiveness of placing an advertisement in each of these media.
    (d) The attitudes of Britons living abroad towards sending gifts to their relatives and friends in the UK and factors influencing them.
    (e) Estimate the likely response from a leaflet/advertising campaign this Christmas.

(ii) Investigate the feasibility of setting up or commissioning overseas agencies to:
    (a) Advertise and handle leaflet and voucher distribution.
    (b) Obtain and service stocking points for leaflets in all the main towns and cities, e.g. travel agents, banks and card shops.
    (c) Develop a leaflet mail-order business to the customers already using the service.

(iii) Investigate the alternative system of advertising and servicing customers overseas by international direct mail from London.

The resources I intend to use to establish the information are:

    High Commissions.
    London Agents of Overseas Newspapers/Media.

Department of Trade and Industry (Export Department).
Overseas Clubs.
Foreign Students in the UK.
London Buying Agents of Foreign Stores.
International Banks.

Summary

I see my long-term ambition of marketing a 'universal' gift voucher internationally best achieved by building up a business relationship with national chain stores in the short term and generating business for them by exporting their own gift vouchers.

I have already devoted some time to looking at the potential market in the UK for overseas stores' gift vouchers and I shall be spending £500 this year in launching New Zealand vouchers to prime UK markets.

I envisage, however, that there are much greater opportunities and bigger markets for exporting UK vouchers to foreign countries. There is no company in the world operating a service which will directly compete and against this background I expect to see rapid unstinted growth in the first two years, dependent, of course, on the advertising budget.

I therefore feel that overseas markets merit a full investigation this summer with a view to launching a campaign in some or all of them in time for this Christmas and thus providing UK chain stores with valuable export business.

Appendix 6.1: Copy of letter from the Reserve Bank of New Zealand

Dear Sir,

<u>International Girogift Ltd</u>

The Reserve Bank has no objection to the scheme as such. Remittances from New Zealand within the general limits referred to by you can be achieved quite simply by utilising a procedure which is currently available whereby New Zealand residents may with little formality effect individual remittances of not more than $20 with a maximum of $100 per person per calendar year.

It is the intention of this scheme that it be used for small payments such as you envisage and it would appear to be quite suitable for your purposes. Trading banks and post offices in New Zealand can deal with applications of this kind.

Yours faithfully,

Chief Cashier

Appendix 6.2: Copy of letter from The Reserve Bank of Australia

Dear Sir,

Exchange Control

We refer to your letter on cash gifts and advise that there is no restriction on the provision of foreign currency from Australia for bona fide gifts to non-residents by Australian residents.

Accordingly, we would have no objection to Australian residents sending gifts to United Kingdom residents in terms of the gift voucher scheme outlined in your letter, either as a reciprocal gesture or on their own initiative.

If your organisation proposed to formalise the scheme by appointing an Australian agent to collect moneys, etc., that agent would need to approach us, through his bankers, for the necessary authority under the Banking (Foreign Exchange) Regulations to enter into the arrangements. Any authority which we might give to the arrangements would be subject to:

(a) applications for periodical remittance to the United Kingdom of funds being supported by schedules showing full names and addresses of donors and beneficiaries and the amount of each gift;

(b) the value of gift remittances on behalf of any one Australian donor not exceeding $A1,000 per annum (amounts in excess of this would need to be the subject of a specific application).

Appendix 6.3: Copy of Letter from Boots Ltd

Mr. R. Senior
Girogift International
32 Valo Close
Harpenden
Herts

Dear Mr. Senior,

Further to our discussion today I would confirm that the discount available
to you is 10% and I note also you will be sending cash with orders. The
discount terms are to stand for twelve months, then reviewed in the light of
the success of Girogift International.

Attached is suggested copy for your leaflet and I think it will sell the
product better than listing merchandise ranges.

I am bound to mention our agreement is subject to a satisfactory reference
from your bank and I feel sure this proviso will not cause you any concern.

Yours sincerely,
for THE BOOTS CO. LTD

S.G. Hope
MANAGER, INCENTIVES & AWARDS DEPARTMENT

Enc.

Appendix 6.4: Draft Agreement with EMI

THIS AGREEMENT is made the   BETWEEN EMI RECORDS
LIMITED of Blyth Road Hayes Middlesex (hereinafter called "EMIR" of the
one part and   of GIROGIFT INTERNATIONAL
(hereinafter called "Girogift") of the other part WHEREAS (1) EMIR operates
a service known as the "EMI record token service" (hereinafter called "the
Service") whereby authorised dealers sell to the public record tokens with
accompanying cards and exchange the same for records to the value of the
amounts shown on the tokens.
      (2) Girogift wishes to buy record tokens and cards from EMIR in
connection with a scheme whereby customers of Girogift living abroad will
purchase from Girogift or Girogift's representatives abroad vouchers pursuant
to which Girogift will forward to designated addresses in the United Kingdom

gifts including EMI record tokens.

NOW THEREFORE IT IS AGREED as follows:–

1.   Girogift will purchase and EMIR will sell record tokens in such quantities
as may be reasonably required by Girogift in books of 20 or 10 as follows:–

    50p in books of 20

    £1 in books of 10

    £1.50 in books of 10

    £2 in books of 10

    £2.50 in books of 10

    £5.00 in books of 10

2.   The price payable by Girogift shall be the face value of the tokens less
10%, payable cash with order.

3.   Record tokens despatched by Girogift shall be attached by Girogift
to official EMIR greetings cards (illustrated or plain). The illustrated cards
may be purchased by Girogift from EMIR at the price of 35p per 10 plus
VAT and the plain cards at 50p per 50 plus VAT. The property and risk in
the record tokens shall pass to Girogift upon delivery to Girogift and EMIR
shall not be required to make any refund or other allowance to Girogift in
respect of record tokens subsequently stolen or destroyed.

4.   It is understood and agreed that in the performance of this Agreement
and in connection with the business of Girogift whether in this country or
abroad Girogift and its representatives shall not be, act or represent themselves
as the employees agents, or representatives of EMIR or any associated
company of EMIR and shall not have the right, power or authority to bind
EMIR or make any contract or other agreements or assume or create any
obligation expressed or implied on behalf of EMIR. Neither shall the making
of this Agreement nor the performance of any of the provisions hereof be
construed to constitute Girogift the agent or the representative of EMIR for
any purpose, nor shall this Agreement be deemed to establish a joint venture
or partnership between parties here. In particular without prejudice of the
generality to the foregoing Girogift shall not whether in connection with
advertising or otherwise use any trademarks or logos, whether registered or
not, used by EMIR.

5.   Girogift shall indemnify EMIR against all costs claims damages and
expenses arising out of Girogift's failure to meet its obligations to its
customers in any way and shall take such steps as may be necessary in
connection with all publicity and documentation to make it clear that
Girogift's customers are contracting with Girogift alone and that EMIR has
itself no liability.

AS WITNESS the hands of the parties hereto the day and year before written

SIGNED by   )

)

)

)

)

for and on behalf of   )

EMI RECORDS LIMITED   )

in the presence of   )

Appendix 6.5: Extract from letter from The Bank of England

Dear Sir,

Under current exchange control regulations and subject to the following conditions, the Bank of England would be prepared to issue an authority for your company to set up the proposed gift voucher scheme which, it is understood, will initially be operated between the United Kingdom and Australasia.

The conditions referred to above are:

1. United Kingdom purchasers of gift vouchers must sign a declaration, on the lines of the attached specimen (questions 4 and 5 of which, you will note, vary slightly from those on the specimen declaration handed to you at the above-mentioned meeting), to the effect that he/she is aware that the value of the voucher(s) purchased will count as a charge against his/her Cash Gift Allowance.

2. Vouchers may not be issued to customers whose answers to questions 4 and 5 of the declaration indicate that they have fully utilised their Cash Gift Allowance for the current year which, in the case of Australia and New Zealand, is presently £1,000.00.

3. Payment for vouchers by your company to the London Buying Office of the non-resident store will not be made before the orders, plus funds, have been received from the United Kingdom resident.

4. The signed application forms − referred to in 1. above − should be submitted to the Bank of England at regular intervals of not more than three months.

5. Any amendment or extension to your company's scheme/mode of operation should be submitted to the Bank for prior consideration.

For your information, we mention that Australian residents are not permitted to send cheques out of Australia unless the specific authority of the Reserve Bank is obtained. Banks in Australia are able to provide drafts, mail and telegraphic transfers etc., expressed in foreign or Australian currency for bona fide gifts.

Yours faithfully,

Sgd.

C.K. Evans
For the Manager
Exchange Control Department

Appendix 6.6: International Girogift Form

Gift Voucher Scheme (Australia and New Zealand)

Bank of England Ref: I/1196 EC 629/C.6		Date:
1. Full name and address of APPLICANT. (BLOCK CAPITALS PLEASE)		
2. Name, address, nationality of BENEFICIARY. (BLOCK CAPITALS PLEASE)		
3. Value of Gift Vouchers required.		
4. Have you made any other cash gifts through the Overseas Money Order Service, National Savings Certificates, Premium Savings Bonds, or through the Post Office or any bank, or arranged cash gifts vouchers under any other scheme, during the present calendar year to any beneficiaries resident in the Overseas Sterling Area as defined below?		YES/NO
5. If the answer to Question 4 is "Yes", does the total of cash gifts, including the present application exceed £1,000.00? (See Note Below).		YES/NO

NOTE:— The value of any gift vouchers provided under this scheme will count as a charge against the donor's Cash Gift Allowance for the current calendar year. Residents of the United Kingdom have a Cash Gift Allowance of a total of £1,000 per calendar year to beneficiaries resident in the Overseas Sterling Area which at present comprises the British Commonwealth (except the United Kingdom, Canada, Gibraltar and Rhodesia), Bahrain, Republic of Ireland, Jordan, Kuwait, Maldive Islands, Oman, Pakistan, Qatar, South Africa and South West Africa, the United Arab Emirates and the Peoples' Democratic Republic of Yemen.

DECLARATION: TO BE COMPLETED BY ALL APPLICANTS.
I DECLARE that:
1. I have not been promised, nor do I expect, reimbursement of this sum in whole or in part from the beneficiary or any third party, whether in cash or in goods or services, and whether directly or indirectly linked with this gift.
2. The Payment is not in discharge of a liability incurred or to be incurred by me or any third party.
3. The information given on this form is true.

I AM AWARE THAT THE VALUE OF THE VOUCHER(S) I AM NOW PURCHASING WILL COUNT AS A CHARGE AGAINST MY CASH GIFT ALLOWANCE FOR 197 .
I UNDERSTAND THAT THE FURNISHING OF FALSE INFORMATION ON THIS FORM IS AN OFFENCE UNDER THE EXCHANGE CONTROL ACT, 1947.

Date ....   Signature of Applicant ....

DISCUSSION POINTS

This is a new idea, but still a service business.
- Does this idea form the basis for a viable business?
- What are the likely threats from competition?
- Has Rod Senior investigated the market sufficiently?

SUBCONTRACTING V. MANUFACTURING: PRECISION ENGINEERING INDUSTRIES*

Summary

Precision Engineering Industries (PEI) was registered as a business name in July 1979. The brainchild of Colin Goss, a trained engineer with management experience, PEI was to be engaged in the manufacture and sale of precision tools, mainly in the plastics industry. Colin planned to develop the business in two stages: PEI Sales would be established to get the idea off the ground and to build up sufficient custom for the second stage. This was to be PEI Manufacturing which in the long term would manufacture moulds for the plastics industry, but would probably begin by undertaking sub-contract milling for smaller mould manufacturers.

Colin approached several government lending agencies, but had mixed fortunes. CoSIRA (Council for Small Industries in Rural Areas), however, were interested in his project and had promised assistance. Determined to set up his own venture, Colin was now faced with some critical decision making:

> I enjoy the challenge of creating organisations and achieving results, although I need to acquire more knowledge about finance and marketing. Most businesses fail by underfinanced, inexperienced people trying to break into crowded markets. To succeed it is necessary to pick an area of operation with a high potential for success and to have the funds and expertise to cope with the start-up period. But I am fairly realistic about this, I think, and am prepared to start slowly and learn as I go, before taking any necessary risks.

The Toolmaking Industry

The toolmaking industry is very fragmented with a high degree of specialisation. The average size of the member companies of the Gauge and Toolmakers Association is 30 and this overstates the situation as a

---

*This case was written by Peter Wilson of the Institute of Small Business, London Business School, and is based on a series of reports compiled by Bob Lovesey.

whole, as the smallest firms tend not to belong to the Association.

There are a number of consequences of this fragmentation:

(i) Small firms limit the scope of their activities by both market sector and product specification.

(ii) Such firms do not invest to any great extent in the training of the necessary craftsmen.

(iii) They tend to have relatively unsophisticated management styles and in particular a limited involvement in sales and marketing.

There are several different processes used to achieve production of components in high volumes at a low cost but to a consistent quality. They include press forming, stamping, coining, diecasting, plastic blow moulding, plastic vacuum forming and plastic injection moulding.

In general terms the industries using these processes are organised in a three-tiered structure. The manufacturer of the final product forms the largest tier, as for example in the motor industry where Ford and General Motors are amongst the biggest companies in the world. Such companies procure many of the components for their cars from medium-sized companies such as Lucas. In turn these companies buy their tooling from the third tier which is made up of very small specialist toolmakers.

Colin's venture was concerned with this last stratum of business and the relationship between the toolmaker and his customers.

Within the industry there are several sectors of specialisation corresponding to the process for which the tools are to be used. Companies will be equipped to make such tools by virtue of the machine tools they possess and the skills of their employees. They will be further specialised by the size of tool they can make, the precision to which they can operate and the materials of which they have experience. In general their business will be based on continuous relationships with a limited number of customers who, being aware of and having confidence in their area of specialisation, will provide a regular flow of repeat work.

Moulds are made up of several parts which when fitted together can be used in a moulding machine to make components to very high dimensional accuracy. This places very high demands on the toolmaker for precision work. The industry suffers from a shortage of toolmakers. At the more sophisticated end of the mould making sector there is a significant international trade. With moulds costing over £30,000 transportation costs are not significant and moulds are exported from

the UK to the Far East and are also imported from Europe.
Colin decided to aim at the sector of the industry which specialised
in the manufacture of moulds for plastic injection moulding. But he
realised that to gain the initial acceptability he needed for long-term
success, he would have to specialise even further.

One of the major problems is that it takes at least five years to train
a toolmaker, although by attracting toolmakers from other companies
many companies can overcome this problem. This tends to drive up the
wages of toolmakers and makes the task of the entrepreneur much
harder. Colin proposed to overcome these problems by training his
labour force over an extended period. This meant that at the outset he
would need to manufacture relatively simply tools until his employees
became more competent.

Colin:

My project seeks to fill a gap in the supply of skilled toolmakers.
Being a professional engineer with industrial training experience, I
have been able to solve this type of problem in the past for previous
employers. I have identified a specific industry where this shortage
is acute and worsening.

An opportunity for doing this existed because many of the smaller
toolmakers subcontract parts of the moulds to relieve the pressure on
their more skilled craftsmen. In particular they subcontract the
surrounding bolster work of the tool, which is made on milling
machines. Colin came to the conclusion that the only way into the
industry, therefore, was to start as a subcontract milling organisation
with specialisation in mould bolster work.

Markets

The plastics processing industry covers a market of about £2 billion a
year in the UK. Some 5,000 companies are involved in the industry, of
which about 29 per cent are mainly concerned with injection moulding.

Many industries are continuing to replace traditional materials with
plastics and this is particularly true of the motor industry where the
plastic content of cars has increased from about 10 kg per car in 1965
to about 90 kg in 1978 (US figures). This is expected to double by
1990. The chief impetus for this is the need to reduce car weight to
improve fuel efficiency.

Colin was confident that the market for moulds and dies had been increasing in sympathy with the growth in plastics consumption (see Appendix 7.1). Although the broad picture painted by the statistics was fairly rosy, Bob needed more qualitative data and to this end he commissioned an investigation of potential customers and end users of plastic products. This was undertaken by two students and their findings are summarised in Appendix 7.2.

PEI Sales

Many of the small toolmakers do not have an active sales policy. They tend to rely heavily on existing customers and repeat business. This very often means that their business is concentrated on a small number of customers, which puts them in a vulnerable position on two counts. First, if one of their major customers reduces demand it can take some time to replace their business and secondly it is likely that their pricing policy is inhibited. Given an aggressive sales organisation, Colin felt that toolmakers could secure more profitable business.

The problem is that the typical toolmaker is too small to support a full-time sales force of his own. Colin recognised that this would be true of the proposed manufacturing company in the early stages. His idea was to establish a separate sales company – PEI Sales – which would establish itself as an agency for a number of toolmakers engaged in mould making.

PEI Sales would be established before and apart from PEI Manufacturing. It would seek to be self-financing by generating income from the sales secured for its client companies. PEI Sales would offer a number of advantages to its clients:

(i) It would be able to seek out more work for the clients over larger markets, including foreign markets, than they could do from their own resources.
(ii) It would be able to secure better prices than companies could themselves.
(iii) It would be able to provide better continuity of work flow by balancing the work between clients.

By July 1979 Colin had already secured the UK and Irish Republic agency for a leading firm of mould makers in Switzerland. He had also established a trading relationship with an established agency in Zurich, which would help PEI Sales to develop its contacts in Europe to achieve UK export sales.

The sales forecasts are given in Appendix 7.3 in the first year cash flow. Assuming the normal commission rate of 5 per cent applies, PEI Sales would need to handle some £720,000-worth of business in the second year. This was the output of about 40 toolmakers. As the average toolmaking company employs about 25 toolmakers, this meant representing twelve such companies and handling something of the order of 15 per cent of their turnover.

PEI Manufacturing

The long-term objective of PEI Manufacturing was to engage in the manufacture of moulds for the plastics industry. As the company proposed to train its own craftsmen, the time taken to do this prohibited an immediate entry to mould making. As described earlier, milling is one process which is frequently sub-contracted, in particular the smaller mould makers tend to sub-contract their bolster work so that they can concentrate on the more skilled aspects of the work. PEI Manufacturing would commence operations as a sub-contract milling service, but seeking to do as much work as possible for mould makers.

The financial appendices are based on the assumption that the manufacturing operation would start with five operatives and a working foreman. They would be equipped with standard Bridgeport milling machines. Ancillary equipment such as cutter grinders would also be necessary.

Factory Location

Location depended on:

Availability of labour.
Availability of financial assistance.
Access to markets.
Access to support services.
Management logistics.

Before deciding on the optimum location, Colin visited several of the development agencies to see what was on offer. These included the

Welsh Development Agency, the Development Board for Rural Wales, the Highlands and Islands Development Board, and CoSIRA. Although some of the incentives available were very tempting, the bureaucracy and rigid requirements as a quid pro quo for assistance were daunting. CoSIRA seemed to offer the best deal with the best possible location being North Norfolk, which was reasonably accessible to the potential markets in the Midlands and South East and within reasonable reach of support services at Norwich, Kings Lynn and Cambridge. The catchment area was big enough to provide a supply of trainable labour but was sufficiently remote from substantial centres of competing employment for a stable pool of skilled labour to be built up.

A factory of about 1,000 square feet would be required at the outset. Discussions with CoSIRA indicated that factory space of this size was included in the 1980 building programme for Fakenham in North Norfolk. As PEI Manufacturing was due to start in late 1980, this fitted in well with Bob's plans.

The Entrepreneurial Team

Colin proposed to run both PEI Sales and PEI Manufacturing. His track record since 1963 covered personnel and training responsibilities with such large companies as Smith's Industries and Raleigh, and he went on to become distribution director of Cassells and eventually administration director of that company. Prior to 1963 Bob had worked as a project engineer, after graduating with a first-class honours degree in engineering in 1961. As a student engineer he worked on the design, manufacture and installation of electrical equipment and systems, and after graduation on rolling mill control systems. In addition, he had held various positions in the Institute of Personnel Management and had been a member of the National Industrial Relations Committee of the Freight Transport Association.

PEI Sales – Sales Manager

For this position Colin proposed to offer participation on a partnership basis to a suitably qualified and experienced person. Discussions had already been held with someone with a degree in plastics technology and who had previously been involved in a company making plastic components and was then sales executive for a plastics importing company. Colin planned to have someone fully involved in the activities of PEI Sales by the end of 1979.

PEI Manufacturing – Production Manager

Colin was looking for an experienced skilled machinist with management experience. He had found someone who fitted the requirements and who displayed a keen interest.

Financial Structure

PEI Sales

Start-up capital was needed to pay salary costs for the full-time employee, his travel expenses and for initial promotional costs. A car would be leased at the outset. In assessing his cash flow needs, Colin assumed that it would take a year to reach the target level of activity. As he was already establishing contacts at that stage, he considered that the ability to generate some cash in the first three months of operation was not unrealistic. A 60-day credit period was assumed.

In the first year Colin estimated that bank facilities would be required for £2,500 working capital in addition to the equity stake of £5,000. The entire equity was to come from Colin himself although he felt that the working employee should have a significant stake in the business.

PEI Manufacturing

For the cash flow forecast and accounts, Colin based his figures on a start-up employing five operatives and one working foreman/director. Some of the operatives would be trainees. A sales value of £8 per operative hour was used and assumed to be generated by PEI Sales. Although a 45-day debtor period was assumed, the industry has a stage payment procedure.

The funding of the company was seen to come from three sources: (i) shareholders, (ii) CoSIRA, (iii) the bank. CoSIRA looked the most promising source. They were limited to towns with populations below 10,000 and to projects requiring less than £50,000 and no more than 80 per cent of total project costs. Their loans were limited to plant and premises, normally five years for the former and 20 years for the latter. Interest rates were set at 3 per cent below base. In some circumstances the loan repayment period could be delayed by one year. Colin assumed that the factory would be rented and the CoSIRA money used for plant purchase. He or his working partner would provide the equity of £7,500. During the first year bank facilities would be needed to cover working capital to a forecast level of £5,250.

Timetable

1 July 1979	Establishment of Precision Engineering Industries.
1 July 1979	Establishment of PEI Sales.
3 July 1979	Agency agreed with Swiss company.
4 July 1979	Agreement made with Swiss agency.
October/November 1979	Target date for appointment of full-time sales manager.
January 1980	Commitment required to factory project.
May 1980	Factory equipment orders placed.
August 1980	Factory Manager appointed.
September 1980	PEI Manufacturing commences production.

Appendix 7.1: UK Manufacturers – Output/Sales of Engineers Small Tools and Gauges

Year	Net Output[a]	
	At current prices (£m)	At 1970 prices (£m)
1963	74,3	98,3
1968	113,7	127,0
1970	152,0	152,0
1971	154,0	139,6
1972	149,0	122,5
1973	198,6	149,4
1974	236,4	155,6

| | Net Sales[b] | |
Year	All enterprises (£m)	Moulds & dies for plastics (£m)
1974	330,1	14,7
1975	388,2	15,2
1976	403,8	16,5
1977	525,4	23,0
1978	621,7	27,5

Notes: a. Gross output less cost of materials, fuel and other minor costs.
b. Excluding VAT, commissions and discounts.

Appendix 7.2: July, 1979 – Investigation Into the Industry of Toolmaking for Plastic Injection Moulding: a Summary

All the interviewed companies were within the London area and were either injection moulders or end users. (By end users it is meant that they assembled plastic parts to form finished articles.) Some end users had their own injection moulding department, others put out such work to separate specialist injection moulding companies.

The following key points emerged from the interviews:

(a) Highly-skilled Toolmakers Are Essential

Toolmaking is a complex and a highly-skilled craft. The tools required for injection moulding are required to be both complicated and accurate. However well managed a toolmaking enterprise, the service it can offer can only be as good as the standard of workmanship produced by its toolmakers. In post-war times there has always been a scarcity of good toolmakers. The problems appear to be that firms are unwilling to subsidise a five-year apprenticeship period and that pay differentials between a toolmaker and an unskilled worker are too low. Firms talk of 'luring a good toolmaker away from his existing company'. The biggest barrier to entry for a new toolmaking enterprise is to find enough labour of a sufficiently high ability.

(b) The End User Has Little Interest in the Identity of the Toolmaker

The end users who do not possess their own injection moulding facilities (i.e. they employed outside injection moulders to produce their components) have little or no idea of the toolmaker who is actually making their tool. They do not exert any influence as to which toolmaker should be used: that issue is left entirely to the discretion of the injection moulder.

(c) Quality of Workmanship When Choosing a Toolmaker Is Important

Most injection moulders choose the quality of the tool as being the most important criterion in assessing a toolmaker. Factors such as cost, reliability and lead times required are secondary to quality.

(d) Good Working Relationship Between Injection Moulder and Toolmaker Is a Key Issue

A key issue in the choice of toolmaker is compatability. With certain toolmakers a relationship develops in which the toolmaker very quickly understands what the injection moulder requires.

(e) Delivery Date Problems Often Occur

There is a great deal of pressure from some end users to demand very low lead times. In order to get the business, toolmakers have to bid tight delivery dates with the result that delays frequently occur. The toolmaker who earns the reputation of meeting short delivery dates will have a considerable competitive advantage.

(f) Mould-design Expertise Is at a Premium

Those people in the industry who can design moulds have a very valuable skill. They combine a knowledge of the exact science of metalworking with the 'black art' of plastic moulding. Such knowledge can only be attained through a great deal of experience: an experienced toolmaker has a significant advantage over his competitors who have to rely heavily on guidance from the injection moulder.

(g) A New Toolmaker Would Find Initial Business

Injection moulders are prepared to try a new toolmaker, but they would wish first to check on his knowledge of the business and on the quality of his workforce and machinery.

(h) Lead Times Vary Greatly But Are Critical

Lead times vary from three to 40 weeks, depending on the complexity and size of the tool. The lead time is usually critical. This is particularly so when multi-component assembly is planned and the mould is required for a critical component.

(i) The Mould Design is Usually the Responsibility of the Toolmaker

The design of the mould has two stages. The first, known as the General Arrangement, or GA, is drawn up very early in the design process. It can be produced by either the injection moulder or the toolmaker but the first draft forms the basis of discussion between the two in which alterations are suggested and changes made until an agreed GA is obtained. The second stage consists of drawing out a detailed design from the GA. It can be a very complex series of documents and is normally the responsibility of the toolmaker to produce. Large toolmakers may possess their own designer/draughtsman. Smaller operations sub-contract a freelance designer.

(j) Some Toolmakers Working Within a Toolmaking Organisation Are Self-employed

A practice which has been operating for many years is for toolmakers working within a toolmaking shop to be classed as self-employed. For the injection moulder, there are tool supply risks associated with a toolmaking operation having self-employed toolmakers in case a toolmaker decides to leave in the middle of a job.

(k) Each Injection Moulder Uses Several Toolmakers

Most of the injection moulders have several toolmaking companies supplying moulds, the average being four to six. They usually have one or two major suppliers from whom they expect a degree of flexibility in meeting job requirements (mainly short deadlines) in return for the cream of the jobs. In turn, each end user has five or six injection moulders with whom he places business.

(l) Toolmakers Are Chosen by the Injection Moulders' Engineering Department

In the small injection moulding companies there is one owner, or two partners, plus the machine operators. In such circumstances the owner places orders with the toolmakers. In the larger injection moulding concerns the technical manager or the toolroom manager liaises with the toolmakers at the specification and quotation stage and places the tooling order.

(m) Repairs and Maintenance Are Done by the Injection Moulder's Toolroom

The larger injection moulders (such as Airfix and Rootes Plastics) have their own toolroom for repair and maintenance work.

(n) There Is a Very Large Variation in Mould Prices

Mould prices vary from £1,500 to £70,000. The two main factors affecting the cost are the complexity of the tool and the degree of accuracy required.

(o) A Closely-knit Industry Exists

The people in, or associated with, the toolmaking/injection moulding industry tend to be there for most of their working lives. They tend to know one another personally and to deal with one another where possible on a personal, informal basis.

(p) Timing of Payments to Toolmakers Is a Consideration

The toolmaker is paid 1/3 of the contract price when the order is placed, 1/3 upon delivery of the tool and 1/3 when final approval of the tool is given.

DISCUSSION POINTS

This case extends the issues discussed in Seamach Engineering. Recognising the particular problems of setting up a sub-contract engineering business, Colin Goss has proposed a particular strategy.

- What are the problems associated with setting up a sub-contract engineering facility?
- Does the strategy proposed by Colin Goss seem viable?
- How does the student evaluate the financial forecasts produced?

Appendix 7.3 (1): PEI Sales Company Forecast Cash Flow Year 1

| | \multicolumn{13}{c}{Month (£)} | | | | | | | | | | | |
	1	2	3	4	5	6	7	8	9	10	11	12	Total
Commission income	0	0	300	600	900	1,200	1,500	1,800	2,100	2,400	2,700	3,000	16,500
Salary costs	750	750	750	750	750	750	750	750	750	750	750	750	9,000
Travel	500	500	500	500	500	500	500	500	500	500	500	500	6,000
Car lease	150	150	150	150	150	150	150	150	150	150	150	150	1,800
Promotion	100	100	100	100	100	100	100	100	100	100	100	100	1,200
Clerical costs	100	100	100	100	100	100	100	100	100	150	150	150	1,350
Directors' fees	100	100	100	100	100	100	100	100	100	100	100	100	1,200
Bank charges					10	20	25	30	30	25	15	5	160
Net cash flow	(1,700)	(1,700)	(1,400)	(1,100)	(810)	(520)	(225)	70	370	625	935	1,245	(4,210)
Equity	5,000												
Opening balance	5,000	3,300	1,600	200	(900)	(1,710)	(2,230)	(2,455)	(2,385)	(2,015)	(1,390)	(455)	5,000
Closing balance	3,300	1,600	200	(900)	(1,710)	(2,230)	(2,455)	(2,385)	(2,015)	(1,390)	(455)	790	790

Appendix 7.3 (2): PEI Sales Company Profit and Loss Forecast

	Year 1 (£)	Year 2 (£)
Commission income	22,500	36,000
Salary costs	9,000	12,000
Travel costs	6,000	8,000
Car lease	1,800	1,800
Promotion	1,200	1,500
Clerical costs	1,350	2,500
Directors' fees	1,200	2,400
Profit before interest	1,950	7,800
Interest	160	0
Net profit	1,790	7,800

Appendix 7.3 (3): PEI Sales Company Forecast Balance Sheet

	Opening (£)	Year 1 (£)	Year 2 (£)
Equity	5,000	5,000	5,000
Reserves		1,790	2,090
Tax			2,500
Creditors			1,000
Dividend			5,000
Total	5,000	6,790	15,590
Assets			1,500
Debtors		6,000	6,000
Cash	5,000	790	8,090
Total	5,000	6,790	15,590

Appendix 7.4 (1): PEI Manufacturing Company Forecast Cash Flow Year 1 (£000)

	\multicolumn{12}{c}{Month}												
	1	2	3	4	5	6	7	8	9	10	11	12	Total
Sales revenue		3.7	7	7	7	7	7	7	7	7	7	7	73.7
Wage costs	2.5	2.5	2.5	2.5	2.5	2.5	2.5	2.5	2.5	2.5	2.5	3.5	30
Materials		1	1	1	1	1	1	1	1	1	1	1	11
Premises			2.5						2.5				5
Promotion	1			1			1			1			4
General costs	.75	.75	.75	.75	.75	.75	.75	.75	.75	.75	.75	.75	9
Directors' fees			1.5			1.5			1.5			1.5	6
Loan interest			.6			.6			.6			.6	2.25
Bank charges			.1			.1							.2
Net cash flow	(4.25)	(.55)	(1.95)	1.75	2.75	.55	1.75	2.75	(1.8)	1.75	2.75	.75	6.25
Equity	7.5												7.5
Term loan	25												25
Loan repayments			1			1			1			2	5
Plant purchase	30												30
Opening balance	32.5	(1.75)	(2.3)	(5.25)	(3.5)	(.75)	(1.2)	.55	3.3	.5	2.25	5	32.5
Closing balance	(1.75)	(2.3)	(5.25)	(3.5)	(.75)	(1.2)	(.55)	3.3	.5	2.25	5	3.75	3.75

Appendix 7.4 (2): PEI Manufacturing Company Profit and Loss Forecast (£000)

	Year 1	Year 2
Sales	84	138
Wages	30	48
Materials	12	19.2
Production O/Hs	3	4.8
Gross profit	39	66
Promotion	4	6
General O/Hs	11	17.6
Directors' fees	6	8
Depreciation	6	9.4
Profit before interest	12	25
Loan interest	2.25	2.6
Bank interest	0.2	0.1
Net profit	9.55	22.3

Appendix 7.4 (3): PEI Manufacturing Company Forecast Balance Sheet (£000)

	Opening	Year 1	Year 2
Equity	7.5	7.5	7.5
Reserves		9.55	31.85
Loans	20	20	21
Tax			
Creditors		1	1.6
Dividend			
Total	27.5	38.05	61.95
Assets		30	48
Depreciation		6	15.4
Stock		4	6
Debtors		6.3	11.3
Cash	27.5	3.75	12.05
Total	27.5	38.05	61.95

8 MOVING FROM MANAGING A BUSINESS TO SETTING UP A NEW ONE IN THE SAME MARKET: EUROBOND LAMINATES LTD*

In the spring of 1980, Mike Ford was approached by Nick Williams and John Hunt who owned, amongst others, a steel stock-holding company.

Nick We know that you are fed up with your current employer and are thinking of setting up your own production facility for composite panels. We have the money and the supplies so why don't we go into partnership.

Aged 30, Mike had worked for his current company for ten years and had progressed to the position of Contracts Manager, reporting directly to the Managing Director. In this position he had built up the composite panels business to the point where it contributed a significant part of total revenue.

Mike I was responsible for the day-to-day running of the division; buying, selling, administration, production, design, technical enquiries, research and development, and health and safety. With such involvement in the business, I was able to identify new opportunities, but our small company was acquired twelve months ago and the new owners weren't interested in this side of the business. I knew that I hadn't enough capital to start on my own, but Nick and Jo changed all that. Also, they were prepared to spend money to give me time to investigate it thoroughly before we finally went ahead. I was a bit worried about the effect on my family of my starting another major project – I had spent seven years first studying for my ICMA and then for my BA with the Open University – but I decided that this was an opportunity not to be missed and so I decided to go ahead. The first thing that I did was to write down all my knowledge and thoughts about the business. This would help me to decide what needed to be done and could form the basis of a venture capital proposal in the future, if we needed further money.

*This case was prepared by Sue Birley on the basis of material supplied by Mike Ford.

Towards the end of the Second World War, the United States Airforce developed the Mosquito aircraft, the first major structure to incorporate sandwich panels. These panels could be designed to give very high strength-to-weight ratios and other useful properties such as sound and heat insulation. The simplest type of sandwich consisted of two thin stiff strong sheets of dense material separated by a thick layer of low density material.

The refrigeration industry was one of the earliest to make extensive use of sandwich panels employing plastic foam cores. These panels allowed improved quality and speed of erection, but more importantly clear span buildings could now be designed, requiring much less structural steelwork than previously. The majority of coldrooms are now built using this technique, and I detected a marked acceleration in the movement of caravan and portable accommodation builders to employ composite construction.

The Product

By initimately bonding thin strong skins to a suitable core material, a variety of semi-structural composite panels, with applications in the building and portable accommodation industries, can be produced. Most panels available are flat; however, the new plant will be capable of producing curved panels which will encourage rainwater run-off.

The physical properties of the product may be varied depending on the properties of the central core and skins. The best model of composite panels is based on standard 'I' beam theory, which I have studied in depth. The overriding assumption of the model requires the bond between the core and skins to be stronger in tension that the foam.

Results I acquired show that conventional contact adhesives cannot attain core breaking bonds on the plastic foams which account for the cores for the majority of insulated panels (see sketch in Appendix 8.1). The major advance in this new product involves the use of a thermoset adhesive which can be shown to give much improved bond strength and heat resistance.

The Market

As the main sales contacts are with cold store builders the initial market will be low temperature food storage rooms both deep freeze and chill.

Based on the estimated sales of BSC white plastic-coated steel for 1980 at 6,000 tonnes, the low temperature panel market will be 750,000 M^2 or £10m/£15m. This estimate is rough, however, as it does not take into account imports and other types of skins, it is likely to err on the low side.

From my knowledge of the market, I estimate that in 1979 it was shared as below:

Supplier	Type of Panel	Share	Volume	Value £m
W.D. O'Gorman[a]	Bonded EPS and styrofoam	11.0	80,000	1.2
C. Hemmings[a]	Foamed PU	10.0	75,000	1.3
Fosters[a]	Foamed PU	10.0	75,000	1.3
Tylers[a]	Foamed PU powder paint plant	8.5	65,000	1.3
Smiths[a]	Bonded PU	8.5	65,000	1.1
Kitsons[a]	Foamed PU aluminium	5.0	40,000	0.8
Cape Building Prod.[a]	Foamed PU bonded EPS	5.0	40,000	0.7
Parklite	Bonded EPS styrofoam PU	5.0	40,000	0.6
Modulam	Bonded EPS PU	5.0	40,000	0.6
C.M. Coote[a]	Bonded EPS	5.0	40,000	0.6

Note: a. Builders and refrigeration engineers who have expanded and mainly supply own contracts.

The balance is made up of a large number of small concerns often making traditional timber-framed panels. These will be the target for special efforts as timber framed panels become too expensive due to the shortage and cost of skilled joiners.

As far as the three main competitors are concerned, Parklite have been weakened as a result of a takeover, O'Gorman's are concentrating overseas and it is rumoured that Hemmings are in some financial difficulty.

Initially sales will come from the following:

1. Contacts — mainly cold store builders.
2. Convert timber frame users.
3. Refrigeration engineers wishing to build own enclosures.
4. Self build by owner (farmer dairyman, freezer centre, etc.).

However, the market potential is huge for the following reasons:

1. Home freezer ownership likely to rise by 5 per cent p.a. to 1983. As this segment purchase three times as much frozen food as non-owners, more freezer centres and cold stores will be required.
2. Modern meat plants are being air-conditioned to meet EEC requirements, this temperature ideally suits the low-cost EPS cored panel.
3. Dry goods stores will be temperature controlled in the near future.

Therefore, it is intended to investigate the following areas for new business:

1. Hot process insulation up to $100°C$.
2. Caravans.
3. Portable accommodation (15,000 units per annum = 1,000,000 square metres).
4. Refrigerated and temperature controlled transport.

Marketing Strategy

I propose to offer a high quality panel with good service and technical back-up. My pricing strategy will be to follow the price leaders for panel sales to independent erectors. Currently, Parklite Insulation hold this position and they will be supported in their moves to increase margins. I will promote through my existing contacts and through advertising and hopefully editorials in trade journals.

Production

The intention is to manufacture large panels up to ten metres long, which needs a large factory area. A layout, as shown in Appendix 8.1, will reduce handling and internal transport, all a one-way stick which will halve the lay-up time. For such a layout I will need a minimum area of 6,500 square feet of factory space with a modern clearspan portal frame assuming all the foam raw materials are stored outside and finished goods are either stored outside or are shipped on completion.

Being a steel-using facility ideally the factory should be sited at Shotten on Deeside. (The conditions for an advance factory from the Welsh Development Agency are shown in Appendix 8.11.) The location is roughly equidistant from the major sources of raw material and is near the M56. It is a Special Development Area and likely to get further assistance from British Steel Industry. I know that factory units will become available from spring 1980.

Finance

The other two directors own a steel stockholding company which will supply 60 per cent of the value of raw materials. Also the working and fixed capital will be provided by this company through credit on purchases, along with bank overdraft and trade credit.

Appendices 8.2-8.10 shows Mike's initial financial analysis, using the following assumptions:

(a) Variable costs   :   Materials and transport
     Semi fixed costs   :   Direct wages and insurance
     Fixed costs   :   Balance

(b) Minimum staff level:

Direct	4 men @ £100 p.w.	20,800
Salaries	Manager and foreman	16,250
	(£8,750) (£7,000)	
Total		37,050

(c) Expected staff level:

Direct	6 men @ £100 p.w.	31,200
Salaries	Manager, foreman, assistant	20,750
	(£5,000)	
Total		51,950

(d) Estimate for grants:

Direct	6 men + accounts clerk +	
	telephonist	37,200
Salaries		20,750
Total		57,950

(e) Rent and rates: These could be reduced to 6,500 sq. ft. if all foam r.m. are stored outside and finished goods are either stored outside or shipped on completion. One possibility is to use trailers and charge customer if delivery cannot be made. Details will have to be on quotations, etc.

(f) Minimum area: 6,500 sq. ft. @ £3.80 = £24,700. Efforts will be made to get a rent free period of 2/5 years.

Appendix 8.1

Bond Lines under a Microscope

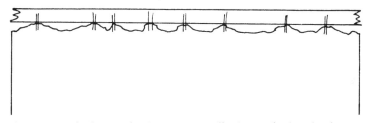

Conventional thermoplastic contact adhesive only bonds the peaks developing less than 80 per cent of core strength.

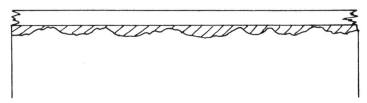

Shaded area represents new liquid thermoset adhesive filling surface cavities before setting and developing 100 per cent bond strength.

Factory Layout

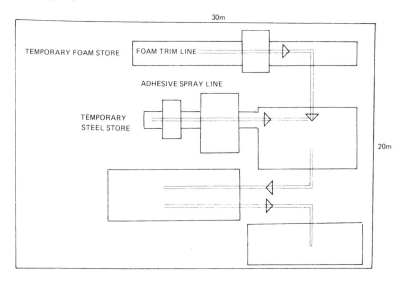

Appendix 8.2: Profit & Loss Account — Minimum Costs Year 1

	£	£
Sales		225,000
Materials and transport	150,000	
Direct labour	20,000	
	170,000	170,000
		55,000
EXPENSES		
Salaries	16,200	
Rent	19,500	
Rates	4,000	
Energy	2,000	
Telephone	600	
Other expenses	13,000	
Interest	2,300	
Depreciation	6,800	
	64,400	64,400
		(9,400) LOSS

PRO-FORMA BALANCE SHEET END YEAR 1

Shares	1,000	Fixed asset	65,000	
Reserves P&L	(9,000)	less depreciation	7,000	58,000
	(8,000)			
Current liabilities:		Current assets:		
Creditors	133,000	Stock	10,000	
Bank overdraft	8,000	Debtors	65,000	
			75,000	
	133,000			133,000

Appendix 8.3: Calculation of Year 1 End Balances

	£
STOCK	
Adhesive	2,000
Work in progress ½ week	3,400
Raw materials 1 week	5,000
Finished Goods	10,400
CREDITORS	
Trade and other materials − sales	16,000
− stock	4,000
Steel	67,000
stock	5,000
Telephone	200
Energy	500
Capital	45,000
	137,700
DEBTORS	60,000
STEEL PURCHASES	
Sales	90,000
Stock	5,000
	95,000
Paid	28,000
Balance	67,000
Additional unpaid capital	45,000
Owe associated company	112,000
OTHER PURCHASES	
Sales	60,000
Stock	4,000
	64,000
Paid	44,000
Balance	20,000

Appendix 8.4: Cash Flow Break-even Minimum Costs Sales £255,100

Item	1	2	3	4	5	6	7	8	9	10	11	12	Total
Inflows													
Shares	1000												1000
Sales	—	—	—	10000	10000	10000	20000	20000	20000	25000	25000	25000	165000
Total	1000			10000	10000	10000	20000	20000	20000	25000	25000	25000	166000
Outflows													
Steel	—	—	—					4000	4000	4000	8000	8000	28000
Trans. & other Mtrls.	—	—	—	2670	2670	2670	5330	5330	5330	6670	6670	6670	44010
Wages	870	1740	1740	1740	1740	1740	1740	1740	1740	1740	1740	1740	20010
Salaries	1350	1350	1350	1350	1350	1350	1350	1350	1350	1350	1350	1350	16200
Rent	1625	1625	1625	1625	1625	1625	1625	1625	1625	1625	1625	1625	19500
Rates			2000						2000				4000
Fuel Power Light					500			500			500		1500
Telephone					200			200			200		600
Monthly expenses	1620	1620	1620	1520	1520	1420	1520	1420	1420	1420	1520	1420	13000
Capital									10000	10000			20000
Balance b/f		(4465)	(10800)	(19135)	(18040)	(17645)	(16450)	(8015)	(4180)	(11645)	(13450)	(10055)	(10055)
Balance	(4465)	(10800)	(19135)	(18040)	(17645)	(16450)	(8015)	(4180)	(11645)	(13450)	(10055)	(5820)	(5860)

Appendix 8.5: Profit & Loss Account Expected Costs Year 1

	£	£	
Sales break even		277,000	
Materials and transport	185,000		
Direct labour	24,000		
	209,000	209,000	
		68,000	

EXPENSES			
Salaries	21,000		
Rent	20,000		
Rates	4,000		
Energy	2,000		
Telephone	1,000		
Other expenses	13,000		
Interest	2,000		
Depreciation	7,000		
	70,000	70,000	
		(2,000)	LOSS

BALANCES			
Creditors	71,000 + 35,000 + 1,900 = 107,000		
Debtors	33,000		
Stock	17,000		

Material and Trans.				
Cost of Sales	33,000	47,000	60,000	67,000
Sales	50,000	70,000	90,000	100,000

STOCK	£Q1	£Q2	£Q3	£Q4
Adhesive	1,000	1,000	1,000	1,000
WIP ½w	2,000	2,000	3,000	3,000
RM 1w	3,000	4,000	5,000	5,000
FG 1w	4,000	6,000	7,000	8,000
Total	10,000	13,000	16,000	17,000

PRO FORMA BALANCE SHEET EXPECTED COSTS YEAR 1

Shares	1,000		Fixed assets	65,000	
Reserves P&L a/c	(2,000)		Less dep.	7,000	
	(1,000)				58,000
CURRENT LIABILITIES			Current assets		
Creditors	107,000		Stock	17,000	
Bank O/D	2,000	109,000	Debtors	33,000	50,000
		108,000			108,000

Appendix 8.6: Cash Flow Break Even Expected Costs Sales £310,000

Item	Total	1	2	3	4	5	6	7	8	9	10	11	12
Shares	1000	1000											
Sales	243000			17000	16000	17000	23000	23000	24000	30000	30000	30000	33000
Total inflows	244000	1000		17000	16000	17000	23000	23000	24000	30000	30000	30000	33000
Steel	48000							6000	6000	6000	10000	10000	10000
Trans. & other Mtrl.	66000			5000	5000	5000	6000	6000	6000	8000	8000	8000	9000
Inc. in stock	17000		10000			3000			3000			1000	
Wages	24200		1700	1700	1700	1700	2200	2200	2600	2600	2600	2600	2600
Salaries	20400	1700	1700	1700	1700	1700	1700	1700	1700	1700	1700	1700	1700
Rent	20000	1600	1600	1600	1600	1600	1600	1600	1600	1600	1600	1600	1600
Rates	4000			2000						2000			
Energy	1500					500			500			500	
Telephone	600					200			200			200	
Other expenses	13200	1100	1100	1100	1100	1100	1100	1100	1100	1100	1100	1100	1100
Capital	30000							10000		10000	10000		
Interest	2000	100	200	300	200	200	200	100	100	100	200	200	100
Total flow	(2900)	(4500)	(16300)	3600	4700	2000	10200	(5700)	1200	(3100)	(5200)	3100	6900
Balance b/f			(3500)	(19800)	(16200)	(11500)	(9500)	700	(5000)	(3800)	(6900)	(12100)	(9000)
Balance	(2900)	(3500)	(19800)	(16200)	(11500)	(9500)	700	(5000)	(3800)	(6900)	(12100)	(9000)	(2100)

Appendix 8.7: STF Panels Ltd Grant Estimates Projected Profit & Loss Account 1980

	1st Q	2nd Q	3rd Q	4th Q
Sales	60,000	80,000	100,000	130,000
Mat. cost & trans.	40,000	53,280	66,660	86,580
GM	20,000	26,720	33,340	43,420
OTHER EXP.				
Direct wages	5,200	6,500	7,800	7,800
Salaries	5,190	5,190	5,190	5,190
Rent	5,000	5,000	5,000	5,000
Rates	1,000	1,000	1,000	1,000
Fuel, power, light, etc.	500	500	500	500
Telephone	200	200	200	200
Audit & accounts	150	150	150	150
Printing & stationery	600	600	600	600
Insurance	600	600	600	600
Depreciation	1,700	1,700	1,700	1,700
Sundry	500	500	500	500
Selling expenses	3,000	2,000	1,000	1,000
	23,640	23,540	23,740	23,740
Net profit before tax	(3,640)	3,180	9,600	19,680
STOCK				
Finished goods 1 wk	5,000	6,700	8,300	10,800
WIP ½wk	2,100	2,800	7,000	9,000
Raw materials 1 wk	3,330	4,400	5,555	7,215
	10,430	13,900	20,855	27,015
DEBTORS	Pay 60 days			
CREDITORS	Mostly 60 days			

Appendix 8.8: Balance Sheet as at End Year 1

Ordinary shares 1000 @ £1	1,000	Fixed assets	65,000	
Profit & loss	28,820	Less depreciation	6,800	58,200
Shareholders funds	29,920			
CURRENT LIABILITIES		CURRENT ASSETS		
Creditors	124,254	Stock	27,015	
Bank overdraft	17,807	Debtors	86,666	
		Cash		113,681
	171,881			171,881

Appendix 8.9: Grant Estimates – Year 1 Cash Flow

Month / Item	1	2	3	4	5	6	7	8	9	10	11	12	Total
Inflows													
Shares	1000												
Sales			20000	20000	20000	26666	26666	26666	33333	33333	33333	43333	
Total													
Outflows													
Steel	—	—	5333	5333	5333	8000	8000	8000	10656	10656	10656	13332	
Trans. & other Mtrls.	1733	1733	1733	2167	2167	7104	7104	7104	8888	8888	8888	11544	
Wages	—	—	—	—	—	2167	2600	2600	2600	2600	2600	2600	
Salaries	1730	1730	1730	1730	1730	1730	1730	1730	1730	1730	1730	1730	
Rent	1667	1667	1667	1667	1667	1667	1667	1667	1667	1667	1667	1667	
Rates	—	—	—	—	—	2000	—	—	—	—	—	2000	
Fuel, Power, Light	—	—	—	—	500	—	—	500	—	—	500	—	
Telephone	—	—	—	—	200	—	—	200	—	—	200	—	
Audit & Acc.	50	50	50	50	50	50	50	50	50	50	50	50	
Printing, Stat. & Post	200	200	200	100	100	—	100	—	—	—	100	—	
Insurance	200	200	200	200	200	200	200	200	200	200	200	200	
Sundry	167	167	167	167	167	167	167	167	167	167	167	167	
Selling expenses	1000	1000	1000	1000	1000	1000	1000	1000	1000	1000	1000	1000	
Capital	—	—	—	—	—	—	—	—	—	—	—	—	
Balance	(5747)	(12494)	(4574)	2912	9698	12279	16327	19775	26150	32525	38109	(17307)	

Appendix 8.10: Financial Analysis of Five-year Running of Panel Plant

Profit/turnover as per projections for BSC industry

CASH FLOWS

	1	2	3	4	5
Capital	(61500)				5,000
Special dev. grant (22%)		13,500			
Tax allowance		5,500	25,250	–	(2,500)
Inc. in stock	(32,500)	1,300	(9,300)	–	40,500
Inc. in debtors	(75,000)	3,100	(21,500)	–	93,400
Inc. in creditors	65,000	(3,100)	(14,100)	–	(76,000)
Profit add back dep.	11,000	56,000	76,000	76,000	30,000
Corporation tax	–	–	–	(38,000)	(53,000)
NPV	(93,000)	76,300	56,350	38,000	37,400
Disc. @ 25% 40,500	(77,500)	53,000	32,000	18,000	15,000
30% 22,000	(71,500)	45,000	25,500	13,000	10,000
40% 10,000	(66,500)	39,000	20,500	10,000	7,000

Debtor/Creditor 60 days each

Appendix 8.11: The Welsh Development Agency Industries Sites and Premises

The Welsh Development Agency was established in January 1976 to help to improve the economy of Wales and in particular to encourage industrial development. The Agency can provide suitable industrial premises and sites for firms which wish to locate in Wales or which are seeking to expand existing activities in the Principality. While the prime concern is to help manufacturing industry, firms which provide essential services to industry are also considered.

The Agency's existing portfolio, of around 450 factories, totalling some 17,000,000 sq. ft. of floor space, includes the major industrial estates at Treforest, Bridgend/Waterton, Hirwaun, Swansea and Wrexham together with numerous individual and group sites in other parts of Wales.

Advance Factories

The Agency has a major commitment to build factories in advance of demand. The factories, which range in size from 1,500 sq. ft to 50,000 sq. ft are designed to be suitable for a wide variety of industrial uses and are built to a high standard of specification. They are located close to available sources of labour and wherever possible are set in pleasant surroundings. There is usually a selection of advance factories ready for immediate occupation and the Agency has a continuing programme to develop further sites.

Purpose-built Factories

The Agency is prepared to build factories to meet an industrialist's own requirements and, taken with extensions of premises for existing tenants, this type of work forms a very significant proportion of the Agency's total building programme.

Ground Leases

The Agency will readily lease sites to industrialists who wish to build their own factories. Fully serviced land is currently available in a number of strategic locations.

Leasing Terms

Factories of standard design and serviced sites are available for leasing at attractive market rentals. Factories are normally let for up to 25 years, with rent reviews at five-year intervals. In most cases, factory lettings attract rent-free concessions for up to two years.

Specialised buildings are normally built only for sale on the basis of a 99-year leasehold interest.

Ground leases may be granted for a term up to 99 years with rent reviewed currently at ten-year intervals.

Assisted Area Incentives

The whole of Wales has assisted area status and therefore offers industry certain attractive financial benefits. These include rent-free periods for Agency factories; Regional Development Grants towards the cost of new industrial buildings and, in most areas, plant and machinery; and selective financial assistance under the Industry Act 1972 for viable projects which will improve employment prospects in the chosen location. The Agency will advise on how to apply for these incentives and works closely with other government bodies to provide a property and financial package best suited to the industrialists individual needs.

DISCUSSION POINTS

Mike Ford reflects similar dissatisfactions to the three partners in Light Engineering. He is leaving his present employment to form a new business in direct competition.

- How many of the skills which he used whilst in employment are transferable?
- How independent will the new business actually be? In other words, what are the personal risks for Mike?
- What further information, if any, would the student need in order to decide whether to invest in the business?

9 FORMING AN EXPORT BUSINESS: N & Z EUROPEAN HI-FI (DISCOUNTS) LTD*

N & Z European Hi-fi (Discounts) Ltd, was a limited company set up in September, 1976 by two people, Zvonko Bencic and Nik Plevan, to deal exclusively with the mail order sale of hi-fi equipment (and ancillary goods) to anywhere in Europe. More specifically, the business was meant to deal especially with Yugoslavia, the country of origin of both the partners and the country of residence of Bencic.

By the end of November 1976, the company was in a position to begin trading and the partners were optimistic about their chances of success.

The Original Idea

Zvonko and Nik had first met whilst working as couriers for separate travel companies in the same hotel in Yugoslavia. They quickly developed a strong bond of friendship and trust, and subsequently visited each other's homes frequently, even though they lived in different countries – Zvonko lived in Yugoslavia while Nik lived in London.

It was Zvonko who first suggested the idea that they should set up a business together. Neither one had any fixed idea of what particular business to go into, but both knew that they wanted to work for themselves.

Several different business ventures were suggested, but the hi-fi business was agreed on because

1. It was believed that a market of real potential existed in Yugoslavia.
2. The capital investment was negligible.
3. Little time was needed to run the business, most of the work being of a clerical nature.
4. The potential rewards were very high.
5. The competitive advantage of running a business dealing with

*This case was written by Nik Plevan under the direction of Sue Birley.

Yugoslavia was significant.
6. Hi-fi was of great interest to both partners.

The Legal Aspects

N & Z European Hi-fi (Discounts) Ltd, was incorporated in September 1976, the legal aspects being dealt with by Michael Pringle and John, Solicitors, of Croydon, Surrey. The reason for forming a limited company was never very clear to either partner, but on reflection they felt that it may well have been the best course of action since a 'good, reputable front' was seen as imperative to sell effectively such an exotic and expensive product. Credibility was of the utmost importance in this business, or in any other where a large monetary outlay was required by the customer.

As there were only two people in the company at the outset, both became directors with a 50 per cent share. Nik: 'We felt that this did not actually mean anything as the company was only a £1 company and there was a gentleman's agreement on the profit share.'

The Marketing Issues

Zvonko lived in Yugoslavia and knew from first-hand experience how difficult it was to purchase good quality hi-fi units in that country. He also knew of the poor reputation that most British firms dealing with Yugoslavia (for example, Lasky's, Henry's, REW and Comet) had there, and that a prompt and courteous service from a new supplier would be received very well by Yugoslav buyers.

Advertising in the usual manner was difficult due to limitations in Yugoslav Law, even if the company had had enough funds for a campaign. Ideally, N & Z would have liked to open a shop in Zagreb or Belgrade but it was impossible in Yugoslavia for any company to be solely an importing concern. Any company involved in importing must also be an exporter, but such companies were not allowed to remain privately owned, as the Yugoslavian authorities like to control the purchase of foreign goods.

Accordingly Mr C. Curcic, a writer in one of the Yugoslav hi-fi magazines, was approached and he agreed to recommend the company to any people who regularly wrote in to him with enquiries about hi-fi systems. These questions were often of a technical nature but were usually accompanied by a request for a recommendation on where to purchase particular pieces of equipment. Mr Curcic also agreed to publish some of the letters in the journals, together with his answers and recommendations, thus adding to the exposure N & Z was to receive in Yugoslavia. For his services, Mr Curcic received some very high quality equipment at a very low price indeed.

Knowing the Yugoslav people, the two partners believed that the promotion and advertising activities mentioned above, together with the incidence and importance of word-of-mouth in the Yugoslav culture, would be sufficient to allow N & Z to succeed in the market, and indeed to prosper.

Suppliers

One of the principal advantages offered by running a mail order business was the fact that very little, if not zero, capital was tied in stock. This naturally meant that no working capital was necessary. However, suppliers were not very interested in a customer who only bought equipment at the rate of one or two per month, let alone one or two per year, as in N & Z's case. Therefore an alternative method of supply had to be found.

Because N & Z had already decided to become Yugoslavia's principal hi-fi supplier, it was imperative that the widest possible range of hi-fi should be available to the company. This of course only made the supply problem even greater. However, Zvonko and Nik spent almost two months talking to all types of hi-fi shops and stores, ranging from Lasky's to the smallest high street dealer, negotiating terms on which these stores would agree to supply them with equipment. Eventually, enough stores had been contacted and agreements signed for N & Z to be able to begin trading with a stock list of equipment at least double some of their major competitors (see Appendix 9.1). Such was the commitment of the business to success that even shops in the USA were contacted; this was felt to be necessary because American equipment unavailable in the UK was very popular in Yugoslavia.

Most of the agreements made with shops were along the following lines. The shop would supply N & Z with equipment of a certain make at a price 2-3 per cent above the trade price at which the shop was being supplied. The shop would pack the goods and stick N & Z labels on the cartons or boxes, then informing the shipping agents to come and collect the goods from the shop. All documentation was carried out by N & Z and sent on to the shop. The shop had a responsibility to give N & Z up-to-date prices which were then valid for one month, this being the time allowed to Yugoslav buyers to make up their minds.

The Practical Aspects of the Operation

The practicalities involved in running N & Z were quite simple, but involved a great deal of standardised forms, and a strict adherance to carefully worked out procedures. The actual course of events during the process of a sale are set out below:

1. An enquiry, stimulated by the letters page in the Yugoslav hi-fi journal, would be received by N & Z.
2. The piece(s) of equipment of interest to that particular buyer would be entered on a special photocopied quotation form connected with the particular shop supplying that make of equipment.
3. That form would be sent to each shop every week (unless valid prices were already known) after enquiries received within that week had all been entered.
4. The form would be returned, with the prices filled in.
5. A sale price to Yugoslavia would be calculated and entered on another special quotation form destined for the prospective customer. This form also had the cost of freight and insurance entered on it, and instructions on the method of payment, account numbers etc.
6. The form would be returned to N & Z if the customer wished to purchase the equipment. The goods would be ordered from the supplier and all relevant export documentation would be carried out, but the goods would not be sent off. The shop was instructed to pack the equipment and send the documents to the client.
7. The bank would then inform N & Z that the money had been received – in Sterling – from Yugoslavia, for what amount, for which goods and from whom.
8. The supplier was instructed to carry on with the shipment, and the insurance forms would be sent on to the brokers.
9. The supplier, insurance broker and shipping agent, would all be paid and the transaction closed.

Sometimes an enquiry would be received from someone who did not know N & Z and the extent of the equipment stocked. In such cases a stock list would be sent first, and an order received later after the prospective purchaser had decided on the goods he wanted.

Financial Issues

As the previous section explains, no money was tied up at any time during a sale. No stock was held, and no bills would come in for payment until the revenue from those transactions was received.

Nik That was the beauty in dealing with a country which realised that it was thought of fairly suspiciously by the rest of the world. I wonder how many people in this country would send off £300-£500 to a foreign country before receiving the goods. But hi-fi is in great demand in Yugoslavia, it is almost a status symbol, and so few people object to these procedures. Furthermore, the UK is held in very high regard in Yugoslavia, and it would be almost unthinkable to a Yugoslav that a British limited company would abscond with his money without delivering the goods first.

Pricing the goods at a competitive level was felt not to be very important since the testimonial in the journal was enough in most cases to convince people that the price was fair. The pricing was therefore done as follows:

Price from supplier	£100
+	
VAT @ 12%	£ 12
Total purchase price	£112
+	
10% profit margin	£ 11.2
Total sale price	£123.2
Profit (after re-fund of VAT)	£ 23.2

PROFIT MARGIN OF APPROXIMATELY 20%

Appendix 9.1

 N&Z EUROPEAN HI·FI [Discounts] Ltd

STOCK LIST

ALL MODELS from the ranges of the Manufacturers listed below are ex-stock

AMPLIFIERS

Accuphase	Lux	Pioneer	Technics
Akai	Marantz	Rotel	Toshiba
Amcron	N.A.D.	Sanyo	Trio
Armstrong	National	Sony	Wharfedale
Bose	Philips	Tandberg	Yamaha
Cambridge Audio	Pioneer	Toshiba	
Cerwin-Vega	Rogers	Yamaha	TURNTABLES
Dual	Rotel		Acoustic Research
Eagle	Sansui	SPEAKER SYSTEMS	A.D.C.
Goodmans	Sanyo	Acoustic Research	Akai
Griffin	Sonab	Aiwa	Bang & Olufsen
Harman Kardon	Sony	Akai	B.S.R.
Hitachi	Tandberg	Richard Allan	Connoisseur
J.V.C.	Technics	Altec	Dual
Leak	Toshiba	Bang & Olufsen	Eagle
Lecson	Trio	B & W	Empire
Lux	Yamaha	Bose	Fons
Marantz		Cambridge Audio	Gale
N.A.D.	TUNERS	Castle Acoustic	Garrard
Naim	Accuphase	Celef	Goldring
Nakamichi	Akai	Celestion	Hitachi
National	Armstrong	Cerwin-Vega	J.V.C.
Pioneer	Cambridge Audio	Chartwell	Leak
Quad	Dual	Dahlquist	Linn Sondek
Radford	Eagle	Eagle	Lux
Revox	Harman Kardon	Ferrograph	Marantz
Rogers	Hitachi	Gale	Monitor Audio
Rotel	J.V.C.	Goodmans	National
Sansui	Lecson	Griffin	Philips
Sanyo	Lux	Hacker	Pickering
Sony	National	I.M.F.	Pioneer
Sugden	Pioneer	J.B.L.	Rotel
Tandberg	Quad	K.E.F.	Sansui
Technics	Rotel	K.L.H.	Sanyo
Toshiba	Sansui	Leak	Sonab
Trio	Sanyo	Lecson	Sony
Yamaha	Sequerra	Lowther	Strathearn
	Sony	Marantz	Technics
RECEIVERS	Sugden	Monitor Audio	Thorens
	Technics	Philips	Toshiba
Aiwa	Toshiba	Pioneer	Transcriptors
Akai	Trio	Quad	Trio
Armstrong	Yamaha	Revox	Yamaha
Bang & Olufsen		Rogers	
Eagle	MUSIC CENTRES	Sansui	CASSETTE DECKS
Goodmans	Aiwa	Sonab	Aiwa
Hacker	Bang & Olufsen	Sony	Akai
Harman Kardon	Goodmans	Spendor	Bang & Olufsen
Hitachi	J.V.C.	Strathearn	Dual
J.V.C.	National	Tandberg	Goodmans
Leak	Philips	Tannoy	Hacker

P.T.O.

Appendix 9.1 (continued)

STOCK LIST (continued)   - 2 -

Cassette Decks	REEL TO REEL TAPE RECORDERS	Philips	Empire
Harman Kardon		Pickering	Fidelity Research
Hitachi	Akai	Pioneer	Goldring
J.V.C.	Amcron	Rotel	Grace
Marantz	Dokorder	Sansui	J.V.C.
N.A.D.	Ferrograph	Sennheiser	Ortofon
Nakamichi	Philips	Sonab	Philips
Neal	Pioneer	Sony	Pickering
Philips	Revox	Stax	Shure
Pioneer	Sony	Technics	Sony
Rotel	Tandberg	Toshiba	Stanton
Sansui	Teac	Trio	Technics
Sanyo	Uher	Wharfedale	Yamaha
Sonab		Yamaha	
Sony	HEADPHONES		OTHERS
Tandberg	Akai	CARTRIDGES	S.M.E. Pickup Arms
Teac	Eagle	Acos	Hadcock " "
Technics	Hacker	A.D.C.	Acos Lustre " "
Toshiba	Hitachi	Audio Technica	Formula 4 " "
Trio	J.V.C.	Bang & Olufsen	Zerostat
Uher	Leak	Denon	Metrosound Equip.
Yamaha	N.A.D.	Eagle	Watts Parastat

THE ABOVE IS ONLY A PARTIAL LISTING OF OUR VAST RANGE OF EQUIPMENT

Please note that there is virtually NO type of electronic equipment that
we cannot supply! If the equipment you desire does not appear in our stock
list, please do not hesitate to enquire on the attached ENQUIRY FORM.
Please also use the Enquiry Form to ask for up-to-date prices of the
equipment listed; hi-fi prices undergo frequent changes in this day and
age so that it is impossible to supply an accurate price list for a range
of equipment as vast as ours.
Amongst other equipment we can supply are televisions, calculators, digital
watches, musical equipment/P.A. systems (M.E.M., Marshall, Hywatt etc.),
video recorders, cassettes, reel to reel tape, professional measuring
equipment, and just about any hi-fi accessory you could want. Gramophone
records (Popular and Classical) can also be supplied at very keen prices
but only in quantities of 20 or more. Please be assured that your enquiry
will be dealt with immediately upon receipt and that goods will be despatched within 24 hours of receipt of order and associated money transfer.

- -

ENQUIRY FORM 1	ENQUIRY FORM 2
To: N & Z European HI-FI Ltd.,	To: N & Z European HI-FI Ltd.,
6, Upper Mulgrave Road,	6, Upper Mulgrave Road,
Cheam, Sutton, Surrey SM2 7AZ	Cheam, Sutton, Surrey SM2 7AZ
Please supply prices on the fol-	Please supply prices on the fol-
lowing equipment:	lowing equipment:
....	....
....	....
....	....
Full Name	Full Name
....	....
Address	Address
....	....
....	....

Appendix 9.2

N&Z EUROPEAN HI·FI [Discounts] Ltd

REGISTERED OFFICE 100, PARK LANE, CROYDON CR9 1DR   REGISTERED NO. 1312999 ENGLAND

6, Upper Mulgrave Road,
Cheam, Sutton,
Surrey SM2 7AZ

Your Ref:

Our Ref:

Dear Mr.

     Thank you for your valued enquiry. We would like to point out that this
letter is a Xerox copy because, by reducing our overheads, we can pass on as much
of the saving as possible to you, our customer. This is equally applicable to our
position on catalogues; we do not supply any catalogues as the high cost of postage,
etc., prohibits this, but then this is reflected in our low, low prices.

Please find enclosed a copy of our current Stock List but, as you will see, there are
no prices quoted and also no model numbers. This is because in a range of equipment
as vast as ours it is impossible to quote accurate prices for individual items at all
times. However, if you would be good enough as to complete the Enquiry Form attached
to the Stock List with the precise models (Make and number) you require the prices
of, we will be pleased to quote you our low prices by return of post. We are proud
to say that our prices have driven many a competitor to lower his prices, and that
we now have the lowest prices in the whole of Britain.

The method of payment is by transferring your money to our account number 50658758
at Barclays Bank Limited, 33 Stafford Road, Waddon, Surrey. Payment must be made in
£ Sterling to our bankers shown above and is best done by telex money transfer
procedure. As soon as the money is received by our bankers, we will ship the equipment
to you within a few days, the transit time to Yugoslavia being in the order of one
week.

We hope that the information given here is sufficient for you and that we may look
forward to the pleasure of handling your first order with us in the near future.

Sincerely yours,

T.A. Burton
Export Department

Appendix 9.3

REGISTERED OFFICE: 100, PARK LANE, CROYDON CR9 1DR   REGISTERED NO. 1312999 ENGLAND

6, Upper Mulgrave Road,
Cheam, Sutton,
Surrey SM2 7AZ

Your Ref:

Our Ref:

Dear Mr.

Please find below the prices of the equipment you requested, together
with the transport and insurance charges.

We look forward to the pleasure of handling you first order with us.

| MAKE | MODEL No. | PRICE £ | TRANSPORT | | INSURANCE |
			AIR	TRAIN (Express)	

T.A. Burton
Export Department

DISCUSSION POINTS

Zvanko Bencic and Nik Plevan have recognised a need in Yugoslavia for modern hi-fi equipment. It would appear to cost them very little to satisfy this need.

- What factors should be considered prior to setting up an exporting business?
- Have they been dealt with in this instance?

10 IMPORTING: LEATHER IMPORTS*

In 1976 Mr Singh approached his bankers for overdraft facilities of £2,000 to finance an import business he had conceived on a recent visit to India. The facility was to be secured by a second mortgage on his semi-detached house. He was a 30-year-old technician with an international drug company earning a salary of about £5,000 and proposed to inject £1,000 of savings into his business.

While in India he had observed that his brother-in-law produced leather goods, for example tooled bags and belts, and sold them on local markets for prices ranging between 20 and 40 rupees (£1 = 15 rupees). He felt sure that similar products were sold in boutiques in London for £20-£30. To test his idea he purchased a few samples and on returning to London confirmed his observations.

After discussing with a few friends who were street-traders the possibility of importing such goods and selling them both on local markets in South-east London and to boutiques, he made arrangements with his brother-in-law to import 1,000 items a month at an average price of 25 rupees. They were to be shipped by British Airways Cargo to Heathrow at a cost of £150 a shipment including insurance. His brother-in-law offered to arrange with his bankers the necessary documentation, insurance and payment. The goods were to be paid for on 30-day sight Bills of Exchange with the arrangement that the documentation giving title to the goods would be released by Mr Singh's bankers against acceptance.

The first shipment was due at Heathrow on 31 March. Mr Singh agreed two days' holiday with his employers to undertake collection and then sell them on a market stall the following Thursday. He was optimistic of selling a couple of hundred items on his first day at prices ranging from £3 to £5, and spoke optimistically of £2,000 profit on each consignment.

*This case was prepared by Stephen Forsyth under the direction of Sue Birley.

DISCUSSION POINTS

Mr Singh has observed that products which can be bought very cheaply in India are apparently selling very expensively in London. A market stall, one day per week, could make a great deal of money.

– What are the factors to consider when importing products for sale?

– What are the key elements for success in a market?

– Does Mr Singh appear to have considered all these?

THE DEAL: THE GREAT BUTTON BONANZA*

One evening in May 1980 John Clark, a man with a reputation for dabbling in a variety of entrepreneurial activities, approached an old college friend who had just commented casually that the company to which he had just been appointed a director with a 'turnaround'-type brief, had a 'wide variety of obsolete stock and other rubbish which they had been trying to get rid of for 20 years'. The result of this approach was a lunch date the next week to see 'the attic'.

The company concerned was a small subsidiary of an engineering conglomerate based in south London making clothing of various sorts but also dealing in zips, buttons and other similar items. It had been in a poor state for some years and was somewhat of an embarrassment to the group accountants who had never been able to sort out a stock valuation with any real meaning.

John quickly realised why there were so many stock valuation problems when he was shown 'the attic'. The area was around 6,000 sq. ft. (he was assured), badly lit, and filled with row after row of dexion-type shelving of various shapes and sizes but averaging roughly 8 ft high and 2 ft 6 ins deep with three shelves. All this shelving was completely utilised and there were further piles of bags, boxes and cartons scattered in the gangways and every other conceivable nook and cranny. A thick layer of dust covered the vast majority of this area and in addition there was an all pervading smell of damp and mould from the various points underneath the site of the frequent roof-leaks.

His colleague was able to tell him that this area had been here for well over 20 years: 'nobody has a clue what there is in any detail. Apparently the original owner had been in the habit of buying job lots from other kindred companies and storing them in the attic on the basis of "they'll prove a good investment one day".' It was also revealed that the company had been trying to sell off the contents for years to anyone who wanted to root around: 'Pay £5 John and you can fill a black plastic dustbin bag with whatever you want, this is how we sell off some of it to market traders. We even had a guy come and fill a whole furniture van for £100 once, but it made no impression as we have so much more junk stock downstairs waiting to be dumped up

*This case was written by John Lambden.

here.' Whilst there were vast piles of zips, belts (non-leather), buckles and other items (that could be seen) 99 per cent of the area was stacked with every conceivable sort of button.

At this moment the storeman arrived to announce that he was going for his lunch in half an hour and wanted to lock up then. Consequently, armed with two plastic bags John spent the next half hour frantically trying to ascertain what there was that might interest him or anyone else. The buttons he found in his mad scramble were of every type — plastic, metal, cloth-covered, glass — with two exceptions which disappointed him; namely mother of pearl and enamel, which he knew could be sold at a high price in the 'antique' world. Moreover they were of all sizes from 1/8 in. to 2½ ins. Every colour was present with a predominance he thought of white, black and brown but it was difficult to be sure. It was so difficult because apart from the poor light, confined space and physical difficulty in getting into the really dusty corners, the buttons were usually in plain white boxes or paper sacks. Ninety-five per cent of the buttons were loose in the boxes but some were carded 6/12/18/24 to a card, ten or twelve to a box. He filled his sacks with these buttons as he saw an immediate market in London around the fleamarkets, if not elsewhere, at the £1-or-so a card for which he had seen them on sale. In addition he found little glass buttons in paper bags of one gross inside boxes (ten to the box). He calculated on one shelf that these boxes occupying an area 3 ft high and 2 ft 6 ins wide contained 1.2 million buttons.

At this point having covered something like 20 per cent of the space the storeman returned to lock up. Having dusted himself down and got rid of some of the dirt on hands, face and clothing, his colleague said to him: 'What do you think John? The whole lot including shelving can be bought for £1,000 book value but you must guarantee to clear the place in three weeks as its our year-end stock-take then and the auditors have insisted on clearance and the landlord wants re-possession.'

'Why are they so cheap? There must be a minimum of a billion [English] buttons here and the racking must be worth a thousand pounds alone' asked John. 'Well, we've tried to sell them for 20 years in the trade and the reason for most of the buttons being here is that they are no longer suitable for automatic buttoning machines, but that won't be a problem to you, will it John?'

DISCUSSION POINTS

This is a case about deals.

- How does the student distinguish between a deal and a business?
- Is the deal offered worth £1,000?
- How many students would like to take it on?
- What would be their strategy for disposing of the assets acquired?

12 THE JOINT VENTURE: JVC LIMITED*

Case A

In March 1980 Keith Adams was talking to his lawyer about the need to find alternative suppliers of aerosol cans for his company Cannes-Hunt. The lawyer, who was based in Cannes, asked his friend Roger Hindle to assist, not realising that Roger was a non-executive director of Hindle Engineering Limited, a small subcontract engineering firm in the UK. Roger Hindle, in turn, asked Peter Tanner, General Manager of Hindle Engineering to investigate the possibilities of setting up a joint venture company within Hindle premises.

Cannes-Hunt (UK) Ltd, and Hunt International (registered in France) were both owned by Keith Adams and Derek Wyatt, Keith being resident in France and Derek in the UK. Their companies operated in the following way. Cannes-Hunt (C-H) bought chemicals for fire extinguishers from ICI and sold the chemicals in their outlets abroad. Some of this chemical was transferred from the ICI containers, by contract packages in the UK, into domestic containers of 1 kg capacity.

There was a gentleman's agreement between C-H and the contract packages that C-H would sell only abroad, leaving the UK market available for their suppliers. There, however, was no formal sales or marketing organisation in C-H. The 1 kg containers were sold by temporary employees, usually students, on a commission basis. The students were given a vehicle containing 5,000 or 6,000 aerosols, and a street map of a town. Selling focused on offices and shops, with orders taken, fire-extinguishers delivered and cash received on the same day. A return visit was usually made to the town after three to four weeks when sales often exceeded the initial level. Sales revenue had been built up as shown in Table 12.1. These figures related to all fire extinguishers but Derek Wyatt estimated that sales of the 1 kg and the new 681 gm units accounts for some 80 per cent of total sales.

The profit on the venture was obviously determined by the prices charged by the contract packager which were £6.00 for 1 kg units and £4.20 for the 681 gm units. However, over the previous six months,

*This case was prepared by Sue Birley on the basis of material supplied by Hindle Engineering Ltd.

Derek Wyatt had become convinced that not only was the delivery response poor, but they were also charging too high a price.

Table 12.1: Sales Revenue

Year	Revenue
1976	£85,847
1977	£250,325
1978	£273,046
1979	£354,543

The Deal

In April 1980, Peter Tanner visited ICI (Runcorn) and the packaging contractors with Derek Wyatt. Peter: 'He was obviously well known by both companies. We had the full treatment – chauffeur-driven car to and from the station, a good lunch etc...' Later that month, after examining the estimates supplied by Derek Wyatt (see Appendix 12.1) Hindle Engineering put forward the following proposal:*

1. Hindle Engineering Limited (HEL) to invest in the plant, create the space and allocate the labour to become a contract packager of aerosols.
2. HEL and Cannes-Hunt to form a joint venture company (JVC) whose role would be to handle the supply of raw materials to HEL and the supply of finished product to C-H.
3. Investment to be as follows:
   HEL – £10,000 for plant ⎫
                             ⎬ £25,000
   HEL – £15,000 into JVC   ⎭
   C-H – £15,000 into JVC
   Therefore, shareholding in JVC to be: HEL 62%
                                          C-H 38%.
4. JVC to sell to C-H at 1 kg   £5.00
                          681 gm   £3.45
   HEL to sell the first 16000 1 kg units @ £3.80 to JVC.
   HEL to sell the first 4000 681 gm units @ £3.20 to JVC.
   HEL to sell all subsequent 1 kg units @ £3.38 to JVC.
   HEL to sell all subsequent 681 gm units @ £2.80 to JVC.
5. The first 5,000 units to be paid for an order.

*Additional calculations by Peter Tanner are shown in Appendix 12.2.

Appendix 12.1: Extracts from a memo to Keith Adams from Derek Wyatt

The aerosol sales in 1979 amounted to 21,793 units of which 60 per cent were for 1 kg units. I estimate that this figure will increase significantly in 1980 to at least 40,000 units. If we were to manufacture ourselves the initial outlay on a small filling machine with a capacity of approximately 400 units per day would be £7,500 for the basic machine plus £1,500 for extra refinements which would help to improve the product. The resultant manufacturing costs would be:

	1 kg	681 gm
Can	0.250	0.230
Valve	0.058	0.058
Actuator	0.016	0.016
Dip tube	0.010	0.010
Handle	0.180	0.180
Mixture	1.330	0.904
Total	£1.844	£1.398

To this must be added overheads, transport, packing materials and labour: say a further 55p. However, if we manufacture, we will require large stocks of all items, therefore we will need about £35,000 as shown below:

	£
Filling machine	9,000
10,000 1 kg cans	2,500
10,000 681 gm cans	2,300
20,000 valves	1,160
20,000 actuators	320
20,000 dip tubes	200
20,000 handles	3,600
Mixture for 10,000 units	11,596
Total	£30,676

Appendix 12.2: Calculations made by Peter Tanner prior to submission of proposal and made available to Derek Wyatt

Labour Costs
At regular production of 200 aerosols per day, two operators would be required to manoeuvre the tanks of BCF, perform the filling operations, checkweigh, package and generally fetch and carry the packaging materials.

Cost per aerosol $= \dfrac{2 \text{ people x 50 hrs per week x £3.20 per hr}}{200 \text{ aerosols x 5 days}}$

 = £0.32

Finance Costs
£22,000 overdraft at 22 per cent, say £2,420 per annum interest charge.

Materials
1 kg = £2.00   680 gm = £1.54

Depreciation
Capital costs anticipated to total £9,000: depreciated over 2 years.

Works Overheads	
Rent, rates, heat, light, power	£8,800
Insurance	500
Telephone	260
Audit and accountancy	180
Post	100
Maintenance	250
Management	1,200
Secretarial	1,000
Canteen, welfare etc.	1,000
Total	£13,290

DISCUSSION POINTS

Case A – Most owners of small sub-contract businesses have a dream of one day having a product of their own to manufacture. Hindle Engineering is given such an opportunity.

- In what ways might the new product fit the existing business?
- Does the business seem viable and what are the potential problems?
- How does the student react to the proposed deal?

Case B

This case reproduces a memo sent by Derek Wyatt to Hindle Engineering in response to the proposal set out in Case A and as a result of a joint meeting between the proposed partners.

1. Costings

The costings have been worked out on the purchase price of parts and gas as supplied by Cannes-Hunt and verified by Mr Tanner. These figures are acceptable.

Depreciation. A figure of £4,500 per annum for two years has been included in the works cost price, which shows as £0.45 per unit.

It is questioned as to whether this figure should be allocated in this manner at all, as the depreciation to Hindle Engineering will in fact be cleared by the payment of £2 over and above the manufacturing cost. The depreciation on the machinery should possibly be carried in the books of the joint venture company.

The same applies basically to the 'Financial Costs' which presumably means the interest on the capital outlay. While this will be a Hindle Engineering cost in the period until the capital is repaid it will, by repayment of a proportion of the £2 for each extinguisher, be on a continuing reduceable sum. Perhaps it requires a complicated formula to take this into account but it would make a difference to the cost figure.

Labour. The cost of labour is shown at £64 for two men per day. This amount seems high and it is the opinion of the writer that Hindle Engineering should charge the joint venture company the actual cost — although the writer would agree that he is not familiar with the Hindle Engineering scales of pay.

Hindle Engineering Charges. The figure shown is £13,290 per annum. It is understood that this includes rent at £8,800 per annum, a sum for secretarial and office work, telephones and a sum for the services of Mr Peter Tanner and Mr David Hindle.

It is felt that the rental, even including rates, is high. It is understood this is in fact the office space. The manufacturing unit will be occupying factory space. Perhaps this figure could be looked at again.

The services of Mr Tanner and Mr David Hindle should, in the opinion of Hunt International, not be costed by Hindle Engineering but should be covered by the share of profits in the joint venture company.

However, it is felt that there is some confusion in the thinking covering the companies involved. It is the Cannes-Hunt thinking that Hindle Engineering will do the actual manufacture, but for the purpose of this venture that part of Hindle Engineering will be considered a sub-section or division of the joint-venture company. In this case the joint venture company should be charged only the actual costs incurred by Hindle Engineering. This figure should include secretarial phone etc. After a time financial costs would not arise for Hindle Engineering as the manufacture would be funded from the joint venture company.

2. Payment for Extinguishers

The request for payment with order for the first 5,000 units is contrary to Cannes-Hunt's understanding of the agreement.

As a compromise it is suggested that for the first five thousand units payment should be on the negotiating date of a letter of credit or 30 days after invoice, whichever is the earlier. After 5,000 units the terms should be 30 days from date of invoice or some such formula. It must be borne in mind that after payment for the first 2,000 units ordered the manufacturing process should become increasingly self-supporting. The continuing repayment of the £2 per 1 kg unit etc., after repayment of the capital investment, could continue until such times as a 'manufacturing' fund has been established in the joint venture company.

3. Despatches from Colnbrook

It is agreed that Cannes-Hunt shall be responsible for despatch of goods from Colnbrook.

4. Invoicing

It is suggested that the invoice date for goods should be the date of despatch from Colnbrook and not the date when they are ready for despatch. In fact there will be little or no difference.

5. Legal Costs

Cannes-Hunt agree the sharing 50-50 of the legal costs in setting up the joint venture company.

6. Anticipated Sales Volume and Shortfall

Cannes-Hunt are willing to agree to a guaranteed take off of 15,000 units in the first twelve months of operation. This should enable the capital investment repayment and funding for manufacture. Therefore no guarantee should be necessary.

7. Dividend Policy

It has been agreed that the joint venture company shall, until the capital investment has been repaid, be divided 75 per cent to the Hindle Engineering partners and 25 per cent to the Cannes-Hunt partners. On repayment of the capital investment the position reverses and becomes 75 per cent to the Cannes-Hunt partners and 25 per cent to the Hindle Engineering partners.

At the point where the Cannes-Hunt partners assume control of the company a policy is required which will protect the Hindle Engineering partners.

It has been suggested that Cannes-Hunt shall pay to the joint venture company a premium (over and above the actual manufacturing costs) of £2 per 1 kg unit and £1 per 681 gm unit delivered, until such time as the capital investment has been repaid and a fund to cover manufacturing costs has been established.

The following suggestions are put forward by the Cannes-Hunt partners as the policy to be followed when the repayment has been made and the manufacturing fund established.

(a) For the following twelve months, Cannes-Hunt shall continue to pay the same premium on each unit as during the repayment period, i.e. the same percentage of the manufacturing cost as the £2 and £1 represent at the commencement.

(b) For the following twelve months this percentage premium per unit shall be three quarters of the percentage premium per unit paid in the period stated in Para. (a).

(c) For the third twelve months and thereafter the percentage premium per unit shall be one half of the percentage premium per unit paid in the period stated in Para. (a).

Such an arrangement will ensure that the joint venture company is profitable.

In order to protect the dividend position of the Hindle Engineering partners the Cannes-Hunt partners make the following suggestions to be effective from the time the capital investment is repaid and the manufacturing fund established. (Although the latter may require revision from time to time.)

1. That 40 per cent of the profit of the joint venture company shall be earmarked for future development and 60 per cent shall automatically be paid as dividend.

2. That to convert the 40 per cent development fund (or part thereof) to dividends shall require the *unanimous* approval of the five partners. To decrease the 60 per cent dividend payment for further development shall also require the *unanimous* approval of the five directors.
3. That without the unanimous approval of the five partners the 40 per cent development and 60 per cent dividend rule cannot be changed.
4. That any invoices presented by any of the partners for consultancy fees etc., shall be deemed to be payment or part payment of their dividend and shall not constitute a cost against the joint venture company (although the books may so show).

DISCUSSION POINTS

Case B — Derek Wyatt has presented his reactions to the deal.
  — What are the students' reactions now?

13 FINDING THE RIGHT MARKETING STRATEGY: PAMAL*

Pamal, a partnership formed to design, produce and market garden furniture, was formed in July 1979 by Malise Graham and his wife Pamela.

Malise:
In the spring of 1979 it was suggested to me that there was a great lack of garden furniture for the small town garden/patio. In May 1979 I went to the Chelsea flower show to see what the competition consisted of. It was here that I had the idea of a container for grow bags, and also a small plain tub for trees outside peoples doors.

The idea was received with great enthusiasm by all who Malise talked to and so he decided to go ahead and set up a facility to manufacture, initially, the growing bag container. Timing was important since he had learnt the majority of growing bags were sold from late April to early June, mainly for growing tomatoes. By February 1980, he had begun to manufacture for stock and he decided to market the containers for the first time by advertising in *The Times* and *The Daily Telegraph* on Easter Saturday. A week after the advertisements had appeared they had received 22 replies, 8 from *The Times* and 14 from *The Daily Telegraph*. All the enquiries via *The Times* resulted in sales, but not one sale was made via *The Daily Telegraph*. Although not totally disheartened by the lack of response, Malise had to decide both whether the marketing strategy he had chosen was correct and what should be his production target for the summer months.

Malise:
The partnership came into being because I have always wanted to start up my own business. I had spent ten years with Montague L. Meyer, a large timber importer and distributor, and whilst with them I spent three years as a management trainee looking into all aspects of timber and plywood importation and distribution. In 1974 I was

*This case was prepared by Sue Birley on the basis of material supplied by Malise Graham.

appointed Manager of their Stamford depot with a staff of about five and a turnover figure of £150,000 per annum, rising to £200,000 per annum. I left the Montague L. Meyer group in November 1978 to start up my own builders merchant in the Vale of Belvoir, but this idea did not take off because we were unable to find an economic site.

The lack of availability of premises continued to be a problem, particularly since Malise required a site which would be suitable for a saw mill. To test out his product idea in the meanwhile a local joiner was asked to make a few items to the Pamal design which were then advertised during November, December and January in *The Garden*, the magazine of the Royal Horticultural Society – 'more as a form of market research than for sales'. The response was very encouraging. Although only a few sales were made, Cyril Fletcher, a well-known broadcasting personality, mentioned the idea and showed the container on television, and the Gardening Director of the John Lewis Group of Stores wanted to exhibit it in their garden for the 'Sunday Times' Competition at the Chelsea Flower Show in May.

In December 1979 a 3,000-square-foot site was finally found on an industrial site in a village called Sewstern, eight miles south of Grantham and very near the A1. On 1 February 1980, a three-year lease was signed, at an annual rent of £4,500, renewable for a further three years. Almost immediately, all the necessary equipment was delivered to the site: a cross cut, a bench saw, a surfacer/thicknesser, a spindle moulder, a router and dust extractors. Along with this £4,000 of stock was obtained from a local timber merchant. On 18 February John Ainger, a carpenter, started work as a machinist. He would also be responsible for staining and packing. Malise estimated that this would provide a capacity of 1000 containers.

Marketing

Malise
  There are over four million growing bags sold in Britain every year and each growing bag has a life of only one year. Of the four million it is known that one million people buy one, and one million people buy two, therefore, if only a small percentage, for example 1 per cent, of that two million equalling 20,000, can be reached a market is available. Furthermore, 80 per cent of the sales are made to people

for growing tomatoes. Indeed, the packaging encourages this and discourages any other use. Geraniums would look very silly planted in an orange and yellow plastic bag with tomatoes on it. Our containers should increase the potential market even further. [See Appendix 13.1.]

It was envisaged that growing-bag containers and the tubs would make the major contribution to turnover in the first years but additional sales would be obtained from selling gardening accessories at agricultural shows throughout the summer. Pamal were committed to about ten in 1980. A review of this form of marketing would be made at the end of the summer before any commitments for 1981 were made. If it was not beneficial then the proposed expenses would be added to the advertising budget.

Whilst it was felt that a large proportion of the revenue would be gained in the summer months, it was of course vital that income should be received during the remainder of the year. It was for this reason that advertising in that period would be directed at the farmer (troughs, and specially moulded timber for maintenance) and the builder (shuttering, as well as small items of timber moulded to pattern so difficult to obtain from a large merchant). It was also envisaged that items should be produced for the Christmas market as well as items to customers own requirements throughout the year, although Malise felt that this should not take precedence over the main function of the company, which was to make garden furniture.

To test the market, Malise had decided to sell his containers by direct mail to the general public rather than to garden centres or DIY stores. He had two main reasons for this choice. First, he did not feel that the manufacturing process was sufficiently organised to deal with the potential large orders which could come from such sources; second, he was not quite sure whether he had priced it correctly, although there was sufficient margin in the price to provide for dealer discounts, should it prove necessary. Since no competition for the growing bag container existed, there was no comparative data, and pricing had been on the basis of 'cost plus'. However, initial feedback from customers suggested that the product might have been slightly overpriced.

The extent to which Malise was able to advertise was limited by the high cost of advertising. He finally decided to place small ads in the gardening section of the following publications:

House and Garden	June	1/8 page	£155
The Garden	May	½ page	£124
The Times	26 April	7cm single column	£70
	10 May	7cm single column	£70
	5 April	10cm double column	£200
The Daily Telegraph	5 April	10cm double column	£500
	19 April	7cm single column	£175
	3 May	7cm single column	£175
Garden News	26 April	13cm single column	£73
Evening Standard	20 May	16cm single column	£260
(Chelsea Flower Show)	21 May	7cm single column	£113
The Observer	18 May	16cm single column	£320
The Sunday Express	11 May	7cm single column	£462

The advertisements invited readers to send for further details rather than money with order. The requirements laid down for direct mail advertisements by the Newspaper Publishers' Association were too stringent for a small, newly-formed business (see Appendices 13.2 and 13.3).

Along with this, press releases were sent out to most of the national papers. By late May, little had resulted from this except an insert in the London 'Evening Standard' (see Appendix 13.4), a mention in the 'Hampstead and Highgate Express' and an article by John Street in the 'Garden News' (see Appendix 13.5). However, Cyril Fletcher had purchased six for his Capital Radio garden at the Chelsea Flower Show late in May and, although he was not prepared to hand out leaflets, he was prepared to pass on any enquiries.

Appendix 13.1: Growing Bag Containers and Tubs

why just grow tomatoes in your grow bag?

Grow bags have all the advantages of an ideal growing medium for most plants but the unsightly PVC bags can spoil the effect. PAMAL have the answer. An attractive durable wooden container, designed for grow bags, that will be an asset to any area, inside or out.

The Cottage, Sproxton, Melton Mowbray, Leicestershire. Grantham (0476) 860266

Photographed, Designed, Reproduced & Printed in England by Fidelity Colour Printers, Basildon, Essex. Basildon 23363/4

Appendix 13.1 (continued)

how do you change the soil in your tub?

The PAMAL Tub has a removable side to facilitate the changing of soil when required without damaging the roots. Stained white to eliminate the problems associated with peeling paint, the PAMAL Tub is hardwood framed for extra durability.

The Cottage, Sproxton, Melton Mowbray, Leicestershire. Grantham (0476) 860266

Photographed, Designed, Reproduced & Printed in England by Fidelity Colour Printers, Basildon, Essex · Basildon 23363/4

Appendix 13.2: Extracts From Details of the Newspaper Publishers' Association Mail Order Protection Scheme

Each new mail order advertiser has to make formal application to the Mail Order Committee and copies of all forms are obtainable from any publication associated with the Scheme. YOUR PARTICULAR ATTENTION IS DRAWN TO THE NOTES AT THE FOOT OF FORM 1 – the questionnaire form which all applicants should take extreme care with when completing. Form 2 requires information about the products to be advertised and it is important to submit advertisement copy (though not necessarily finished artwork) with the application. A sample of the product is sometimes required. Applicants MUST also forward with their application their latest audited accounts/balance sheets since failure to do so may cause delay in processing the application.

On receipt of the application the Mail Order Secretariat undertake a complete credit survey of the applicant and this normally takes about 28 days to complete. The application is then placed before the Mail Order Committee at the first available meeting for consideration and the applicant is informed as soon as possible or the applicant's advertising agency advised if one is employed.

Fees

Before considering an application the Committee will require payment of the appropriate fee and your remittance, made payable to Newspaper Publishers' Association, should therefore accompany the application forms. The fees are payable annually and the Scale which is in operation from 1 April 1980 to 31 March 1981 is as follows:

Advertising Expenditure (in Publications Associated with the Scheme)

			Fees £
Under		£750	75
£751	to	£1,500	100
£1,501	to	£3,000	200
£3,001	to	£5,000	300
£5,001	to	£10,000	500
£10,001	to	£25,000	800
£25,001	to	£50,000	1,100
£50,001	to	£100,000	1,400

£100,001	to	£250,000	1,800
£250,001	to	£500,000	2,200
£500,001	to	£1,000,000	2,600
Over		£1,000,000	3,000

It should be noted that all mail order advertisements are monitored by the Mail Order Secretariat and expenditure is calculated at current rate-card prices. It would therefore be appreciated if advertisers who begin the year in a low bank of the Scale pay the additional fee as they progress up the Scale to keep administrative costs to the minimum. The Secretariat do not wish to be involved in too much correspondence regarding non-payment of fees.

NO FEE IS REFUNDABLE AND ALSO MAY NOT BE CARRIED FORWARD TO THE FOLLOWING FUND YEAR, except in those cases where advertising failed to reach the anticipated expenditure for which the original fee was paid and written application will have to be made to the Mail Order Committee for their approval of either refund or carrying forward of fees.

Appendix 13.3: Names of Publications Associated With the Scheme

Daily Express	The Observer Colour Magazine
Daily Mail	The Sun
Daily Mirror	The Sunday Express
The Daily Star	Sunday Mirror
The Daily Telegraph	The Sunday People
Evening News	The Sunday Telegraph
Evening Standard	The Sunday Times
The Financial Times	The Sunday Times Colour Magazine
The Guardian	The Telegraph Sunday Magazine
News of the World	The Times
The Observer	

Appendix 13.4: Insert in the London *Evening Standard*, Friday 18 April 1980

BAGS OF DISGUISE

If all your gardening is done in pots and tubs, you may like to know that an enterprising firm called Pamal at Sproxton, Melton Mowbray,

Leicestershire, have designed a white wooden container for the gro-bag, which although invaluable, is pretty garish to look at.

These containers cost £28 delivered, which sounds a lot of money, but might be worth it if you have strong feelings about looking at brightly coloured plastic.

Appendix 13.5: Article From *Garden News*, 31 May 1980

What's New

Prettier Face For Growing. The inspiration for the Pamal Grow Bag Container came from two sources – a church bazaar and the Chelsea flower show.

Pamal stands for the partners in a 'Mr and Mrs' firm making wooden flower tubs and garden furniture – Pam for Pamela Graham and Mal for Malise her husband. When they were looking round the Chelsea flower show last year, Malise came to the conclusion that growing bags are a great convenience – but they are ugly.

And he was right, for the more the manufacturers try to disguise that ugliness, with pretty pictures on the packet, the worse they look; it would be better if the whole thing were in some natural shade or even just dirt-coloured.

The obvious solution has been found by Malise Graham. He realised that if a growing bag was to be presentable it needed some sort of covering. Then he remembered a cunning device he had seen on his mother's dressing table, bought at a church bazaar – a fancy container to hold paper tissues, all dolled up with frills and furbelows, to disguise the basic tissue box.

Malise saw the need for a growing bag container, remembered the paper tissues holder, saw how it might be achieved, and so designed the Pamal Grow Bag Container.

It is cut to fit the standard growing bag and is approximately 40 ins x 18 ins x 8 ins (1m x 45.5cm x 20.5cm). The container stands on four short legs and is covered with a lid which has a rectangular hole cut to fit the opening in a standard growing bag.

The whole thing is stained white, not painted, so it will keep its colour longer and not flake off. Furthermore, the stain allows the grain of the wood to be seen, which adds to its attraction.

The container is large enough to take a growing bag or any bag trays. The only trouble is that there is no way you can fill this without removing the lid – but it might well be worth boring a hole in it and positioning the growing bag so that it allows water to be poured through the hole into the tray.

There are no doubt many among you who, like me, use growing bags solely for the purpose of saving space in the garden. If the tomatoes or peppers, perhaps, can be grown in growing bags on a path this will make room for something else which needs a longer and deeper root-run.

It doesn't matter whether the grow-bags are ugly or beautiful – they are essentially utilitarian, for the most part, not even seen.

Out of Sight

So why pay £28.00 (inclusive of VAT, packing and carriage) for a Pamal Grow Bag Container, when it will be out of sight?

True enough. But consider those thousands of people who garden on balconies of flats or who have only a patio for a garden.

A Pamal Grow Bag Container is very much for them. They can fill it with a bag for bulbs in the early spring and replace it with another growing bag for summer bedding plants. And a growing bag is not only an easy way to bring soil to the hanging garden of the balcony, but it is an equally easy way of removing it.

The Pamal Grow Bag Containers are available from Pamal, The Cottage, Sproxton, Melton Mowbray, Leicestershire LE14 4QS. Tel. Grantham (0476) 860268.

Appendix 13.6: Year 1 – Forecast Cash Flows

	FEB	MAR	APR	MAY	JUNE	JULY	AUG	SEPT	OCT	NOV	DEC	JAN	TOTAL
CASH INCOME		500	500	3000	3000	2000	1000	500	500	1000	500	5000	17500
DEBTORS													
TOTAL INCOME		500	500	3000	3000	2000	1000	500	500	1000	500	5000	17500
STOCK			4000	200	200	1000	1000	700	300	200	200	300	8100
EXPENDITURE	400	300	200	200	200	200	200	200	200	200	200	200	2700
REPAIRS	50	50	50	50	50	50	50	50	50	50	50	50	600
WAGES	460	460	460	460	460	460	460	460	460	460	460	460	5520
RENT & RATES	380	380	1380	380	380	380	380	1380	380	380	380	380	6560
TELEPHONE & ELECTRICITY		200			800			800			800		2600
TRANSPORT	200	300	300	300	300	300	300	300	300	300	300	300	3500
BANK LOAN	130	130	130	130	130	130	130	130	130	130	130	130	1560
ADVERTISING	100	600	700	700	600	500	500	200	200	400	400	400	5300
SHOWS				200	150	150				500	500	500	2000
INSURANCE	750												750
TOTAL EXPENSES	2470	2420	7220	2620	3270	3170	3020	4220	2020	2620	3420	2720	39190
EXPENSES LESS INCOME	(2470)	(1920)	(6720)	380	(270)	(1170)	(2020)	(3720)	(1520)	(1620)	(2920)	(2280)	21690
OPENING BANK	(2470)	(4440)	(11240)	(11050)	(11510)	(12880)	(15120)	(19100)	(20940)	(22910)	(26220)	(24380)	
INTEREST	50	80	190	190	200	220	260	320	350	390	440	410	3100
CLOSING BANK	(2520)	(4520)	(11430)	(11240)	(11710)	(13100)	(15380)	(19420)	(21290)	(23300)	(26660)	(24790)	24790

**Appendix 13.6 (cont'd): Pamal Cash-flow Analysis —
Notes to cash flow**

Income

First year no credit sales therefore no debtors, sales made on a cash on delivery, mail order, or retail sales at agricultural shows.

Stock

High for the first year, 46 per cent of sales, this is due to an initial stockholding, which will have to be large to obtain a good price, in conjunction with a low turnover figure. The stockholding drops to 33 per cent and 34 per cent of turnover in years two and three.

Expenditure

A sum allowed for incidentals such as stationery, coffee and milk, although on the high side it was thought prudent to have some leeway on this item for unexpected expenses; for example, no allowance has been made in the cash flow for professional services.

Repairs

Predominantly saw maintenance but it also includes repairs to machinery. The building is insured structurally.

Wages

One man, John Ainger, starting at £4,500 per annum, payable weekly and includes employers' contributions. There is an allowance for the employment of another person in 1981 if deemed necessary.

Rent and Rates

Rent fixed at £4,500 per annum for three years. Rates not yet known but believed to be in the region of £2,000 per annum. Allowance for £3,000 per annum in 1983.

Telephone and Electricity

Includes an ansafone as well as the normal telephone charges. All machines will be powered by three-phase electricity. This figure is an estimate and adjustments can be made to it early on.

Transport

Includes the running of two cars doing a total mileage of 30,000 per annum. Approximate rates:

first year	.11p per mile;
second year	.16p per mile;
third year	.20p per mile.

Bank Loan

On the lines of the National Westminster Bank's Business Development Loan, repayed on a regular reducing basis and interest at 7 per cent equals an effective rate 14.2 per cent. Loan − £11,000.

Advertising

The Garden furniture trade being seasonal most advertising will take place in the summer. The year-round advertising is aimed at bringing custom in all the year round.

Shows

Committed for the year 1980 and a review will take place at the end of the summer to evaluate the success. If found not worthwhile, the budget for the future years will be added to the advertising budget.

Insurance

An estimated figure that may need readjustment, will include full insurance for employee and product liability. It also includes our share of the structural insurance as stated in our lease.

Interest

Calculated on the total monthly overdraft at one twelfth of 20 per cent, hopefully the rate will fall.

VAT

All sums are shown exclusive of VAT for which Pamal is registered.

Appendix 13.7: Forecast Profit and Loss Account

	YEAR 1	YEAR 2
Sales	17,500	85,000
Less Cost of Sales:		
Stock	8,050	28,050
Other Overheads	31,090	40,070
	(21,640)	16,880

	YEAR 1		YEAR 2
10% IMPROVEMENT			
Sales	19,250		93,500
Less Cost of Sales:			
Stock	@ 46% £8,855	@ 33%	£30,855
Other Overheads Constant	£31,090		£40,070
Total Overhead	£39,945		£70,925
TOTAL	(£20,695)		£22,575
20% IMPROVEMENT			
Sales	21,000		102,000
Less Cost of Sales:			
Stocks	@ 46% 9,660	@ 33%	33,660
Other Overheads Constant	31,090		40,070
	40,750		73,730
TOTAL	(19,750)		£28,270
30% IMPROVEMENT			
Sales	15,750		76,500
Less Cost of Sales:			
Stock	@ 46% 7,245	@ 33%	25,245
Other Overheads Constant	31,090		40,070
	38,335		65,315
TOTAL	(£22,585)		£11,185

DISCUSSION POINTS

Matching sales and production is one of the nightmares in any new business. It is particularly difficult in a seasonal business. Malise Graham has had poor results from his first marketing effort.
  – Was his marketing strategy correct?
  – What should his production target be for the next six months?

14 MATCHING MARKETING AND PRODUCTION: THE OMNICLOCK*

Case A

Summary

In 1974 David Jones applied for a provisional patent on his invention, a clock that could be read from any direction. The idea evolved over the years through a number of prototype stages, until in 1978 David decided to produce an initial batch of 100 as a 'limited edition'. Having taught himself all the basic manufacturing skills, he was able to complete 30 clocks towards the end of 1978, which were sold to private individuals for £60 each. The business had reached a critical stage after consuming some £10,000 of David's resources without showing much return, for now a further complication threatened the launch. In April 1979, David, a dentist in a small partnership, decided to set up his own surgery. Thus he was caught in the middle of launching two independent and very different businesses.

David:
Having been the initiator of the idea, then having become competent in about ten trades over two to three years towards production, I felt the thread of tenacity was suitable to steer a new business through the inevitable problems. The difficulties that seemed to be most important were the optimum form, structure and direction of the business including marketing strategy.

The Product and its History

The clock could be produced in three basic forms: a sphere, a cone and a cylinder. Initially, David settled on the cylinder (see Appendix 14.1) but the choice of driving mechanism (battery or mains), visual display (analog with hands, projected light analog and digital), colour and materials could still be varied according to market acceptability. The basic cylindrical product could be easily adapted to the other shapes.

*This case was written by Peter Wilson of the Institute of Small Business, London Business School, and is based on a series of reports compiled by David Jones while on the New Enterprise Programme at the London Business School.

In fact, prototypes of both conical and spherical shapes using a variety of colours were produced with 75 per cent of the components in the basic product. The spherical prototype used an internal light source where the numbers and the moving hands were projected onto the surface of the globe. In short, the basic idea had many variations and could be extended to a number of different uses. Although the Omniclock was intended for domestic or promotional use it had a functional application in large areas such as in station concourses, where the principle of universal display made it ideally suited to open public places.

Some features of the clock were:

- a quality image;
- a quartz mechanism for accuracy and reliability;
- mouldings for strength and consistency;
- use of brass hands (classical clock materials);
- simplicity and elegance with modern appearance;
- a multi-functional image, ranging from the conventional clock to a decorative piece of furniture or object of curiosity;
- to satisfy this curiosity, the clock could be handled easily;
- mass-produceable components and easy assembly.

A British patent was granted for the universal display concept and the US patent applied for. Patents were also applied for in Canada, Japan, Germany, France and Holland, although these had not yet been examined. In total, David estimated he had spent some £5,000 on patent applications and £10,000 on R & D over the past four years.*

By April 1979 the Omniclock was in its definitive production stage and the main problem was seen as a launching strategy. There were no clear plans to introduce large batch production, although David vaguely believed that within six months the first batch would be ready. It soon became apparent, however, that there were still problems with product development, notably the hands, which were made of brass and were difficult to shape, and certain gear moulds, which David had fashioned himself. Also the clock had not been tested over a long period of time, therefore its reliability as a composite working unit was unproven. Finally, David had some doubt as to the consistency and effectiveness of the design of the cylindrical prototype – the outer casing was clear moulded plastic which itself was in some ways inconsistent with the

*The business was incorporated in 1978.

quality image, while the fascia of the clock possibly required a new graphic image.

The Market

Before April 1979 there had been a generally positive response to the Omniclock.

> David:
> The people at the Design Centre were enthusiastic when I showed them [in 1976], but at that stage it was too early; one of their requirements is that at least 100 should be in production. In 1977 I approached NRDC. They thought it was a promising idea and would have taken it on had I come to them earlier, before I had got patents on the way and done most of the development. Five different agents or distributors have wanted to be involved with the project and through one of them the prototype clock was shown at the 1977 trade exhibitions in Birmingham, Paris, Frankfurt and New York. Delivery in one year was specified and at a wholesale price of £12. Even so the distributor received 400 orders and there were serious enquiries by mail order firms in the USA.

In addition, a limited marketing campaign was undertaken from David's surgery and over a few weeks had produced sales of 30 clocks, and a favourable reaction. David saw his target market as people with high discretionary spending, probably the professional and executive classes. Another segment that he intended to exploit was company promotional sales. For example, he proposed to offer the Omniclock to Dunhills with their logo and colours for use as promotional items or as in-house furniture. There was no shortage of possible outlets and there was every indication that the product was in demand.

A certain amount of free advertising had been arranged. On television, 'Tomorrows World' had shown some interest while free editorial space had been promised in eight newspapers and magazines.

Production

By the time the first production prototype was ready, David had perfected a number of his own production techniques, including the manufacture of moulds for the gears and the printing process for the numerals on the clock face. But there were some 33 components and about ten suppliers (Appendix 14.2) in addition to David's own production and it was the goodwill of a few of the major suppliers that had enabled him to purchase small quantities at favourable prices.

The largest moulds had been made professionally but the ten that David had himself made would probably last only for a batch of 1,000 to 2,000 mouldings. The techniques of mould manufacture were learnt over the years, largely as a result of his outside interests and through a sculpture course attended in 1973. Also David had worked as a 'semi-professional carpenter' from 1965 to 1968. His parents were both artists and David ascribed his ideas and practical bent in some way to his background and the moral support given by his family.

Production took place at home and the limited edition batch of the Omniclock was assembled on the kitchen table! His immediate plans were to complete the remaining 70 of the limited edition and sell them at £60 each. Unit costs were about £10 and each clock took about five minutes to assemble.

David hoped to produce the first production batch of 1,000 units by September 1979 at a cost of between £8 and £10 a unit. The components, some of which had to be bought in, required varying supply lead times and there were minimum order quantities too. Taking advantage of economies of scale would have reduced unit cost to £6 for batches of 5,000 to 10,000 units.

But there were still several production problems. The clock hands were technically the most difficult to perfect. There was no similar product on the market at the time and the solution required under-standing from first principles. In the early stages David hoped that technology or techniques would catch up and provide a solution. Much of the initial development work was wasted — in 1976 an engineering firm tackled the problem and failed; David wrote off to 50 companies with detailed diagrams but this yielded nothing; then he tried to develop a spring-making machine and mandril that would enable him to pro-duce the hands, but this failed too. Eventually he engaged a production research firm in February 1979 who later assured David that the hands would be available in production batches of 1,000 by August 1979 at a unit cost of 40p. A reserve supplier had been identified who could build the hands in small batches at a unit cost of £2 but at shorter notice.

By April 1979 David had almost exhausted his funds in registering patents and developing the Omniclock, except for a small overdraft facility of £2,000, which had been arranged on the basis of a personal guarantee through his surgery. Further production would require external financing, he thought.

The obvious preference is through the bank under personal guarantee – this is where dentistry is useful – however that source would probably not reach £5,000, so my present attitude is to try to think around borrowing the above amounts elsewhere.

David Jones trained at Guy's Hospital Dental School where he qualified with the BDS and LDS in 1974. Thereafter he worked as an assistant to a principal dentist on a part-time basis in order to pursue outside interests. In 1977 he set up with a partner in their own surgery, working three days a week to allow himself sufficient time to devote to the Omniclock as well as to such activities as motor-cycle design and engine development. (David was 1978 South Midland Champion driving a 650 cc supercharged sidecar outfit.)

This was the uncertain position in which the Omniclock and its inventor found themselves in April 1979. And the future?

David:

The most significant problem I am now facing regarding my own venture is the launch of the clock on a mass-produced basis at home and for export. The will and tenacity which has served well up to production is, however, not sufficient when forming the framework and strategy in an international market. In order to make the most of a British invention – to produce a successful launch – I need to co-ordinate the two main factors: marketing and finance.

DISCUSSION POINTS

Case A – Developing new products can often take a great deal of time and, indeed, in some cases, many years. David Jones has produced the Omniclock in his spare time and using his own personal funds.
- What problems has David encountered in producing the Omniclock?
- Could some of these have been avoided?
- What possible marketing and production strategies could he adopt and which one should he choose?
- What contingency strategies would the student suggest?

Appendix 14.1: The Omniclock

Tilthurst Ltd. presents

THE OMNICLOCK

4-Dimensional Space and Time Sculpture

The Omniclock is an entirely new design using a unique principle of display, while retaining the accuracy and reliability of a QUARTZ movement.

A self-displaying product with wide consumer appeal for gift and novelty department.

World Pats. Pend.

The Omniclock is the result of more than three years intensive research which has resulted in a fascinating clock of unique design, but unlike any other clock, it can be read from absolutely any direction.

By combining the patented visual display with its elegance and simplicity, the clock becomes an outstanding focal point when placed on a coffee table or desk, as part of the central furnishing of home or office. At the same time it has the accuracy and reliability of the latest QUARTZ battery operated mechanism.

The cylindrical face uses the same principal as a conventional clock, i.e., the wide hand reads hours direct and the narrow hand reads minutes in units of five, but the sets of numbers are positioned so that one full set of twelve is always visible.

The clock is attractively presented in black with white numbers and gold finished hands. The transparent case is made of scratch-resistant Diacon which is optically more satisfactory than glass.

The Omniclock is extremely simple in operation. It has a quartz movement which is operated by a popular size of battery that can be easily replaced by removing the holder in the central support. The hands are set by simply pressing in the battery holder and rotating it. The entire clock is manufactured in the UK.

The Omniclock is currently available in the cylindrical design as shown, but individual clocks can be especially commissioned in conical or spherical shapes of any size, with mechanisms and colours as required.

SPECIFICATION

O.A. Height	—	143mm (5½")
O.A. Diameter	—	100mm (4")

Battery Type	—	MN 1500
Battery Life	—	approx. 1 year
Quartz Accuracy	—	2 minutes per year

Appendix 14.2: Components for Production Model

MOULDINGS
Case
Base and plug
Face
Top face
Minute bearing
Minute collet
Second collet
Hour bearing
Hour collet
Battery tube end
Battery tube cone
3 gears
1 gear plate

SPRINGS
Battery spring
Central spring
Support spring

HANDS
Minute hand spiral plus 2 legs
Hour hand spiral plus 2 legs

SUPPLIERS
ISC
Dorfern
J. Smith
Fabrisearch
S & M
Smiths Industries
Pudney Cropping
Dow Printing Services
Applied Packaging
Albanian Press

MISCELLANEOUS
2 mechanism holding screws
Battery tube
Battery label

PACKAGING
2 polystyrene packs
Carton
Guarantee form

Appendix 14.3: (1) Profit and Loss Account for the year ended 31 December 1978

	(£)	(£)
Production	2,151	
Less stock	452	1,699
Expenses		3,246
Loss for period		1,547

(2) Balance Sheet for the year ended 31 December 1978

	(£)		(£)	(£)
Share capital	2	Fixed Assets		
Director's loan	2,646	Machinery		542
	2,648			
Less loss for period	1,547	Current Assets		
	1,101	Stock	452	
		Cash	107	559
				1,101

Case B

By July 1979 David had seen several potential customers and their reactions are given in Appendix 14.4. The overall impression gained was promising, with almost everyone interested in the concept, but somewhat hesitant about the design. David discovered that general acceptance was not forthcoming largely because he was not able to show the actual production model. Also at that time VAT was being increased to 15 per cent and summer sales were in progress, with the result that retailers were being cautious and would not place orders. Of those who would, a possible retail price of £49 was mentioned, wholesaling at £25.

But production problems with the gear mould persisted and the R & D consultants had put back completion of the mould to October 1979. There was still no news about the production facilities for the hands.

Better news came from Barclays Bank. They agreed a £4,000 overdraft facility, backed by a personal guarantee, on the basis of the cash flow forecast and pro forma accounts for the year (Appendices 14.5 and 14.6). These projections were based on a small-scale launch with the proceeds of the first batch financing future batches. This strategy stemmed from David's motivations, which he explained as:

> a desire to retain personal control over the development and launch in the early stages; ultimately to avoid involvement with the manufacturing process; to end up running a new product design company; and to minimise any further financial injections. In the early phases of the project it has been essential to be involved with the research, development and manufacture of the product. However, in the mid-term I see the direction of involvement moving towards development of design and marketing, with the production being sub-contracted.

But events soon overtook David. Although he had the entire fascia re-designed with a tinted cover replacing the colourless cover, in March 1980 there was bad news about the production of the hands. It was impossible to get them produced in the quantities required for the launch and David had to look elsewhere.

David:
Since December 1979 I have had to go back to the drawing board. I may have hit on a sequence of different techniques which would give ten hands per day with excellent accuracy as well as potential for mass production. The techniques involve spring bending, heat

treating and chemical passification on a mandril, followed by glueing of the ends. It may seem odd to say this in the light of the above, but I have never wanted to do any of the development or manufacture myself but if nobody else can, one has to!

The Dental Surgery in North London was opened in January 1980 and has consumed much time and money. David had to concentrate on the surgery and its launch necessitated giving up the Omniclock for a time. The future looked uncertain now after 6 years of hard work. Would the Omniclock ever be launched or was it still-born?

DISCUSSION POINTS

Case B — How does the student evaluate market response?
— To what extent are David's own motivations determining the direction which the business is taking?
— What strategy does the student think he will adopt and does it differ from that which he should adopt?

Appendix 14.4: Response of Buyers After Initial Meetings

PETER JONES (John Lewis)	Have been selling classical clocks for years, do not need new ones. (Can chase up and interest.)
SELFRIDGES	Interested, likely to order one or two.
HABITAT	Leaflet sent – not suitable.
HEALS	Interested, need promotion sample, probably small order.
HARRODS	Interested but problem of styling and that the gift department is next to clocks.
LIBERTY	Interested, come back with production sample.
DICKENS & JONES	Too busy with VAT and sales.
HOUSE OF FRAZER	Not able to be seen.
JOHN BARKER	Not yet seen.
MAPLES	Liked but not for Maples.
RYMAN CONTRACTS	Liked it, ordered one.
DAVID HICKS	Interested, too low market.
SAATCHI & SAATCHI	Advised promotion market not suitable.
UNIROSE	(Premium Gifts) too expensive.
BRITISH HOME STORES	Liked – too expensive – later.
DUNLOP	Interested needs redesigning.
GENERAL TRADING CO.	Did not like it.
PRESENTS	Liked, needs colour and price.
ZARACH	Interested, need to be seen again.

Appendix 14.5: The Omniclock – Cash Flow Forecast 1979/1980

	MAY	JUN	JUL	AUG	SEPT	OCT	NOV	DEC	SUB TOTAL	JAN	FEB	MAR	SUB TOTAL	TOTAL
SALES ON 100 BATCH*				1500	1500	1500								
SALES ON 1000 BATCH** 40%						2250	2250	2250	6750	2250			2250	
30%							1700	1700	3400	1700	1700		3400	
30%								1700	1700	1700	1700	1700	5100	
TOTAL SALES				1500	1500	3750	3950	5650	16350	5650	3400	1700	10750	27100
EXPENSES ON 100 BATCH	200													
DIRECT EXPENSES ON 1000 BATCH — MOVEMENTS £10/UNIT				3000										
MATERIALS 3.50			1500	2000										
PACK PRINT .50					500									
TOOLS 1.00		400			500									
TOTAL DIRECT 8.00	600	400	1500	5000	1000				8500					
INDIRECT COSTS — CAR	100	100	100	100	100	100	100	100	800	100	100	100	1100	
PHONE		60			60			60	180			60	240	
INTEREST				40	110	180	220		550				550	
LEGAL		60			60			60	180			60	240	
PROMOTION				250			250		500				500	
CONTINGENCY	50	50	50	50	50	50	50	50	400	50	50	50	550	
TOTAL INDIRECT	150	270	150	440	380	330	620	270	2610	150	150	270	3180	
TOTAL EXPENSES	750	670	1650	5440	1380	330	620	270		150	150	270		1168
CLOSING BALANCE 100% SALES	(750)	(1420)	(3070)	(7010)	(6890)	(3470)	(140)	5240	5240	10740	13990	15240		
75% SALES	(750)	(1420)	(3070)	(7360)	(7590)	(5100)	(2720)	1210	1210	5280	7660	8740		
50% SALES	(750)	(1420)	(3070)	(7760)	(8390)	(6870)	(5490)	(2960)	(2960)	(260)	1290	1870		
500 BATCH 100% SALES	(750)	(1420)	(2320)	(3760)	(3640)	(1370)	(20)	2510	2510	5160	6810	7390		
75% SALES	(750)	(1420)	(2520)	(4170)	(4450)	(2830)	(1950)	(120)	(120)	1830	3030	3410		
50% SALES	(750)	(1420)	(2320)	(4510)	(4900)	(4280)	(3900)	(2770)	(2770)	(1520)	(770)	(620)		

Notes: *Remaining 75 of limited edition at £60 each. **Produced Aug/Sept selling Oct-March at £22.60 each.

Appendix 14.6: (1) Pro Forma Profit and Loss Account for the year ended 31 December 1979

	(£)	(£)
Production		16,350
Closing stock	808	
less opening stock	452	356
		15,994
less cost of sales		8,500
		7,494
less indirect exp.		2,610
Profit for year		4,884

(2) Pro Forma Balance Sheet for the year ended 31 December 1979

	(£)		(£)	(£)
Share capital	2	Fixed assets		
Directors loan	2,646	Machinery	542	
	2,648		1,298	1,840
Profit for year	4,884	Current assets		
	7,532	Stock	808	
		Cash	4,884	5,692
				7,532

15 THE TECHNOLOGICAL BREAKTHROUGH: RES COMPONENTS LTD*

Introduction

In May 1976, Dr Tom Wills was on his way to a meeting with the Investment Manager of the merchant bank MC Cinti Ltd, and at the same time was recapping the facts that he intended to present in an attempt to gain backing of between £70,000 and £90,000 to form a company to both manufacture and sell components for use in vehicle braking systems. The proposed company would be called RES Components Ltd.

The Initial Product

The initial operation of the new company would be based on the production for sale of friction materials. A friction material was usually a moulded mixture of asbestos, rubber and other minor ingredients consolidated at high temperatures and pressures to form friction elements of the required shapes. Table 15.1 gives the composition of a typical friction material together with the respective moulding conditions necessary to produce the element. Friction elements were used as automobile and truck brake linings as well as autovehicle and industrial clutch facings.

The manufacturers of friction elements all employed the same basic technology. Ingredients were weighed out in the relevant proportions (see Table 15.1) and thoroughly mixed in a powder blender.** The mixed ingredients were then pressed into briquettes of convenient size and shape before being placed in a heated mould. The mould was closed, clamped in a press, and the material cured at a high temperature and pressure. When the material had been cured to the extent required, it was removed from the mould and heated for a further period at normal (atmospheric) pressure. The top surface and sides of the element were then ground to the required shape before being spray painted.

---

*This case was prepared by Raymond Shaw.
**These powder blenders are readily available from reputable polymer processing equipment manufacturers.

Table 15.1: Example of a Friction Material Formulation and Moulding Conditions[a]

	% by weight
Nitrile rubber	5
Phenolic resin	11
Graphite	3
Lead sulphite	10
Brass	10
Barium sulphite	12
Aluminium oxide	3
Asbestos	46
Total	100

Note: a. Moulded at 180°C for 15 minutes at 350Kg/cm^2 pressure and then post-cured at 200°C for 20 hours at atmospheric pressure.

Each friction element had to meet preset performance specifications relevant to the purpose for which it would be used. These specifications related to:

1. Noise level when brakes were applied.
2. Rate of wear of elements under relevant braking conditions.
3. The material's resistance to slipping (i.e. its effective coefficient of friction which will usually be between 0.3 and 0.4 μ).
4. The sensitivity of the friction element's coefficient of friction (when measured against cast iron) to:
     (i) temperature of the cast iron disc over the range from 0°C to 60°C;
     (ii) applied brake pressure;
     (iii) speed at which the cast iron discs were revolving.

Due to the large number of vehicle types, there were a large number of different specifications to be complied with, and the manufacturer would normally have a range of around 20 formulations.

The Marketing Opportunity

In 1976 there were only nine companies supplying friction elements in the UK. These nine manufacturers, together with their parent companies, are identified in Table 15.2. (Financial information on certain manufacturing operations is presented in Appendix 15.1 at the end of the case study.) These manufacturers made up the membership of the British Friction Material Manufacturers Association.

Table 15.2: Suppliers of Friction Materials in the UK

Friction Element Manufacturers	Parent Organisation	Notes Concerning the Parent Organisation
Autela components	Automotive Products Associated Ltd	Sales turnover £69m (1975) 11,000 employees Authorised capital £15m
Belaco Ltd & Ferodo Ltd	Turner & Newall Ltd	Sales turnover £240m (1975) 38,000 employees Authorised capital £80m
Brake Linings Ltd	(Independent)	450 employees (1977)
Don International & Trist, Draper Ltd	Cape Industries Ltd	Sales turnover £70m (1975) 7,000 employees Authorised capital £5m
Mintex Ltd	BBA Group Ltd	Sales turnover £67m (1975) 7,000 employees
Gandy Ltd	Allied Polymer Group Ltd	Sales turnover £34m (1975) 6,500 employees Authorised capital £6m
H.K. Porter Co. (GB) Ltd	H.K. Porter Co. Inc. (USA)	Sales turnover $300m (1974) 8,000 employees

Table 15.3 shows the cost breakdown for two disc brake pads which were then being manufactured by a European company with a turnover in the order of £10 million per annum.

Table 15.3: Cost Analysis of Two Types of Disc Brake Pad

	Price (pence)	
Backplate and wasted material	5.3	5.3
Friction material	1.8	4.3
Adhesive	0.1	0.1
Paint and printing	0.7	0.7
Packaging	0.6	0.6
Weighing and mixing	0.1	0.3
Sandblasting (backplate)	0.2	0.2
Preforming	1.1	1.3
Moulding	1.3	1.8
Post curing	0.1	0.1
Grinding	0.6	0.6
Painting, control, packing	0.6	0.6
Material cost	12.5	15.9

To put these cost figures into perspective, the ex-factory price of four brake pads for the Ford Cortina Mark III was £1.80 and the retail price was £6.90. In the case of a commercial vehicle brake lining, if the retail price was £12 for four elements, the factory price would be about £3. The UK market for friction elements for use on automotive vehicles could be split into three segments:

1. Original equipment to the vehicle manufacturers.
2. Replacement parts sold to the vehicle manufacturers.
3. Replacement parts distributed via garages and specialised retail outlets.

All three of these segments pertained to all four types of autovehicle, i.e. to motor cycles, automobiles, tractors and commercial vehicles.

A recent market survey had found that the buyer's choice of a particular brand of friction element was influenced by:

(a) price;
(b) availability;
(c) range of products manufactured by the same company;
(d) perceived image of the manufacturing company as influenced by advertising and the vehicle manufacturers use of the particular brand as original equipment on vehicles.

Advertising by friction element manufacturers was aimed specifically at the purchasing officers within the retailing organisations, with very little aimed at the final customers, apart from that in the form of sponsoring motor racing teams.

Appendix 15.2 depicts the state of the UK auto vehicle market over the period 1970-5 as reflected by the production of motor vehicles in the UK during the period. A forecast ahead to 1980 is also included. Appendix 15.3 illustrates the UK friction element production levels and the level of imports of friction elements into the UK for period 1973-5.

The Potential Entrepreneur

Tom Wills was 28 years old, married with two children. He had a PhD and BSc in Polymer Science and Technology plus two years' experience working for a European friction element manufacturer as head of their research section. In October 1975, he had returned to England to follow a course in Business Studies. Consequently, he considered he had the ideal technical background and business training with which to embark on a venture such as this.

His intention, with respect to this venture, was to form a company which would, in time, become the industry leader with respect to the technology employed in the area of vehicle braking systems and clutch systems. Initially the company would be based within a Special Development Area in the UK, predominantly manufacturing and selling friction elements. In rough figures he estimated that the initial investment shown in Table 15.4 would be required to give him a production capacity of 25,000 pads per week, single-shift working.

Table 15.4: Estimated Plant Cost of the New Company

Plant	(£)
1 powder blender	4,000
9 presses	40,000
Weighing machines, moulds, grinders	20,000
	64,000

If it were to prove possible, Dr Wills would prefer to use the £40,000 (assigned above for the purchase of nine conventional presses) to develop four fully-automatic moulding machines. These would be built from weaker (and therefore cheaper) materials than those used to construct the presses employed at present in the manufacture of friction elements. The automatic machines would employ the principles of 'teledynamic moulding' which involves subjecting the material being moulded to high-frequency vibrations rather than the usual method of subjecting the material to stable high pressures. At the same time this would reduce his manufacturing costs considerably as it would mean employing one operative less. There was also the possibility, at the time, that Dr Wills might be able to interest the National Research Development Corporation into partially sponsoring the development of the automatic moulding machines in exchange for royalties on each friction element sold by the company. Appendix 15.4 shows extracts from an NRDC booklet explaining its methods of funding research and development.

Short-term Objectives

In the short run, Tom Wills considered his target market with respect to friction elements to be as follows:

1. As supplier of replacement friction elements to owners of Japanese cars under the recommendation of the Japanese car manufacturers. In 1975 the Japanese manufacturers supplied 107,922 cars to UK buyers (nine per cent of the total UK new car market in that year). This represented the importation of some 800,000 friction elements worth approximately £2 million.

Dr Wills held the view that the political advantage falling to the Japanese car manufacturers by their switching to European-made replacement parts at the very time when they were coming under increased pressure to reduce exports to Europe, would more than compensate for any sacrifice of financial advantage derived from using Japanese replacement parts. According to Wills' calculation, the particular route into the market would lead to sales of approximately 2,500,000 friction elements per year valued at about £2 million for sales via retail outlets and £100,000 for sales through the manufacturers' outlets. With this in mind Dr Wills had been in contact with one Japanese car manufacturer, with a positive result in that they stated they would be pleased to evaluate the commercially manufactured products, provided the price was competitive (see Appendix 15.5). This greatly reassured Wills who was confident that he could manufacture friction elements at a lower unit cost than any other manufacturer.*

2. This sector included the large petrol companies and motor car component manufacturers. These companies sell, for example, tyres and fan belts under their own brand names. Dr Wills hoped to be able to persuade these and other suitable retailing organisations to carry RES Components's friction elements under their own brand names.

3. The size of the total friction element replacement market was reckoned to be worth around £150 million (1976) per annum (at retail

---

*Because of the limited size of the target market, it seemed unlikely that members of the British Friction Material Manufacturers Association would retaliate en bloc. Even if one of the established producers decided to attack this segment of the market in competition with Tom Wills, he felt sure that the other members of the Association would restrain such unilateral action in case it led to lower price levels across all sectors of the market.

prices) for all vehicle types, i.e. buses, trucks, cars, motor cycles and tractors. There was an outside chance that Dr Wills' ex-employers would soon be going out of business. Various reports from ex-colleagues did not paint a rosy picture of the situation with respect to that company. Staff members had not received a rise in salary in the last two years, even though they had been subject to an inflation rate of 13 per cent per annum in the cost of living, and as a last desperate resort a new managing director had been appointed, without much success. In the case that that company should fail, its agents in Britain and in other countries would be faced with a gap in their product range. Consequently, Dr Wills anticipated entering into some arrangement with these agents in case such a situation did materialise.

Appendix 15.6 shows two advertisements which appeared in the 'Sunday Times' in the week prior to Dr Wills' appointment at M.C. Cinti. From the limited negotiations Dr Wills had with representatives of these companies, both were enthusiastic at selling Wills' brake pads in the UK and overseas if they could be produced at a wholesale (or ex-factory) price of £1 for four elements. In this case, both representatives judged that they would sell as many pads as RES Components could produce. As a result of these conversations, Tom Wills put together a cash-flow statement based on an average sales price (ex-factory) of £0.25 per element. This is reproduced here as Appendix 15.7.

In the situation where Dr Wills had secured the Japanese car manufacturers' approval for his products to be used as replacement parts in their cars, he would use this as a way of promoting his products. He intended launching a concentrated campaign based on radio advertising aimed at convincing the final customer of the technical superiority of his product compared to the competitors' products. The advantage of using radio was that it was much cheaper than advertising on television and also that it seemed ideal as a medium for addressing the company's target clientele, i.e., automobile enthusiasts and car owners who carried out their own car maintenance.

Longer-term Developments

Tom Wills: 'The typical friction element contains some 46 per cent by weight of asbestos. Periodic rumblings are emerging with growing frequency over the health hazard of using so much asbestos in brake components. Some time in the future I hope to be able to introduce friction elements which I have developed and which do not contain any asbestos. At the moment there does not appear to be any great advantage in introducing such a product unless public opinion – as expressed in tighter controls on the use of asbestos – made this obligatory. I retain this belief even though these new elements have demonstrated better braking characteristics than similar elements containing asbestos.

'Spare manufacturing capacity will be taken up by moulding pistons, as used in hydraulic brake cylinders, from highly filled thermosetting plastic resins. These pistons are being individually machined from brass in order to pass the very tight technical specifications brake system manufacturers demand. However, by using the 'teledynamic moulding technique' I have been able to manufacture these pistons from highly filled resins, to technical specifications which have not been possible using the conventional moulding techniques. I have had talks with one of the major British brake system manufacturers who were enthusiastic about the idea of using such products in their brake systems. However, they were unable to commit themselves until they had thoroughly evaluated pistons produced on a full-scale production set-up.

'The second phase of product development within the company will be a regenerative braking system in which the energy dissipated as heat in conventional brake systems during the braking operation would be recovered and subsequently used to propel the same vehicle. The development of a full-scale working prototype of such a regenerative brake system would be financed by the profit the company would make from its friction element operation and would, in the long run, become the company's biggest profit-generator. I estimate the fund required to develop such a system will be £250,000.

'I have in fact already worked out the principle on which such a brake system could be based, which relative to systems proposed by other designers is light and easy to incorporate on combustible fuel-propelled vehicles already in circulation. Charles Cook of the 'Guardian', wrote an article in December 1975, in which he reported that a braking system capable of recovering 28 per cent of the fuel costs of a vehicle was equivalent to a saving of £450 per year if fitted to a London Taxi. I estimate that my particular design would be capable of saving upwards of 50 per cent of a petrol-driven vehicle's fuel costs. Considering there are 28,000 taxis in the UK.

'The production of specialist gaskets and other polymer based articles on short production runs would also be undertaken on a marginal cost basis. An example of such products is the rubber gaskets used in aircraft engines, which although still being used, are no longer being manufactured. As the engines cannot be used without the necessary gaskets, and the cost of a replacement engine is so high, the sale of the gaskets would not be price-sensitive. This would require customers to contact the company rather than the company being involved in a major marketing campaign. Consequently, this would necessitate the company having an established reputation for this type of service and therefore developing a working relationship with the Rubber and Plastics Research Association, as they would be the first suppliers of these products. This operation would involve an additional investment of no more than £6,000.'

Appendix 15.1: Financial Information on Certain Manufacturing Operations (Figures in £,000)

	Gandy Frictions Ltd 1975	Trist Draper Ltd 1974	Trist Draper Ltd 1975	H.K. Porter (GB) Ltd 1974	H.K. Porter (GB) Ltd 1975
Fixed assets	n.a.	1,543	1,941	383	360
Inv in subsidiaries	n.a.	n.a.	n.a.	n.a.	n.a.
Stocks + WIP	n.a.	1,450	1,538	165	200
Debtors	1,223	1,325	1,384	393	412
Cash	n.a.	13	128	21	21
Trade creditors	21	840	960	248	285
Amounts due to parent and fellow subsids.	1,136	1,253	1,175	163	198
Provision for tax		–	–	n.a.	n.a.
Bank overdraft	54	–	–	90	45
Tax A/C	11	425	670	–	–
Provision for dividend	11	–	–	n.a.	n.a.
Loans	–			296	176
Share capital	£2* only	414	414	577	577
P + L reserve	–	561	622	(444)	(311)
Other reserves	–	1,400	1,738	–	–
Sales	2,247	5,328	6,160	1,374	1,895
Gross profit	n.a.	n.a.	n.a.	212	340
Profit before tax	22	323	193	89	179
Profit (loss) after tax	11	128	61	58	123
Exports	n.a.	1,071	947	n.a.	166
No. of employees	n.a.	n.a.	n.a.	206	206

*only two shares issued at £1.

Appendix 15.2: Motor Vehicle Production in the UK

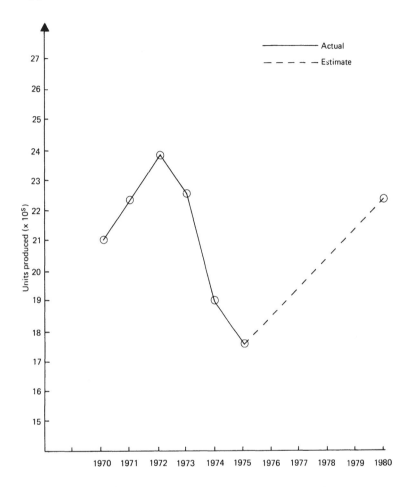

Note: Figures for 1976-80 are estimates produced by the Society of Motor
Manufacturers and Traders Ltd

Appendix 15.3: Friction Elements: UK Production and Imports

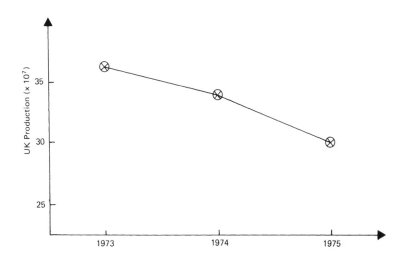

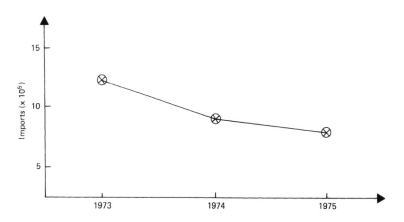

Note: Imports as a percentage of UK production: 1973: 3.0%; 1974: 2.5%; 1975: 2.3%.

Appendix 15.4: NRDC Methods of Funding Research and Development

How the Scheme Works

Funding. Advances are made by the NRDC to the sponsored company monthly or quarterly against invoices relating to an agreed percentage, which can be 50 or more, of expenditure on an approved programme of work.

Recovery. As from an agreed date, levies become payable on the proceeds from commercial sales or usage of the particular product, process or services at a level which, in the event of success, will give NRDC the return of its capital with fair premium related to the risks inherent in the project, or possibly
– levies at a lower rate on the overall turnover of the sector of the company to which the project would contribute, or
– any combination of these two judged to be appropriate, bearing in mind any spin-off benefits which may accrue, even in the event of project failure.

Levies. Levies can be either at a flat rate, time-limited or open-ended, or structured in accordance with actual sales performance, time or any combination of the two, judged to be most compatible with the resultant net project cash flow.

Eligibility for NRDC Finance

Proposals are first screened to ensure that
– they are aimed at a genuine advance in technology,
– even though advanced, they are not merely defensive, i.e. intended to keep pace with established competition.

Given the green light on these scores, a more rigorous assessment is carried out, based primarily on information provided by the client, by which the NRDC seeks to establish that
– the company will be able to meet its share of the costs of completing the proposed programme,
– technical and management resources are equal to the task to be undertaken,
– adequate protection exists for any proprietory rights to inventions or know-how which might be involved,
– the project can, in the event of success, yield a reasonable return on investment in relation to the risk involved.

Appendix 15.5: Letter From Japanese Car Manufacturer

NISSAN MOTOR CO., LTD.

17-1, 6-chome, Ginza, Chuo-ku
Tokyo, Japan

January 8, 1976

Mr. Tom Wills, B.Sc., PhD.,
101 Beatty Road
Stanmore
Middlesex
England

Dear Mr. Wills,

Thank you very much for your letter of 24th December 1975, addressed to our Chairman, Mr. Kawamata.

In the light of increasing export of Datsuns to European countries, particularly to the U.K., and of the political and economic climate in some of those countries, we very much appreciated the ideas that you had advanced in your letter.

As far as the friction materials such as brake lining are concerned, it has been our company policy to recommend to our distributors and dealers that they should use Nissan's genuine replacement parts since they are critical safety-related items. We have not had the occasion to test friction materials manufactured and marketed in Europe to see if they conform to our standards and specifications. We feel, however, that such tests should be conducted so that those replacement and service parts which meet our standards can be purchased provided that they are competitively priced. Availability of such locally manufactured parts will also benefit the Datsun owners in Europe as well.

During the last couple of years Nissan has made efforts to increase its procurement of British-made automotive parts and components. Last spring the representatives of 21 British auto parts manufacturers under the aegis of your SMMT had visited us. We have also received letters of inquiry from 38 British auto parts manufacturers. Unfortunately, in checking the estimates submitted by some of those companies, none could offer us their products at competitive prices.

On the other hand, 18 of our supplier companies have been under license from British manufacturers, and among whom are 3 companies under license from

Girling and one each from Ferodo and Auto Products to manufacture friction materials and brake-related items. Some of our Datsuns being shipped to your country are also equipped with tyres made by the Dunlop joint venture in Japan.

If you are considering setting up a new company to manufacture friction materials and other items to be used for replacement parts for our Datsuns, etc., the most crucial question will be whether you can manufacture such items at competitive prices even if the volume is not too great.

I hope that my comments will be of some use to you in formulating your future policies and in planning your new company. Thank you again for writing us.

Sincerely yours,

M. Goto
Manager
International Advertising &
Public Relations
Export Division
and
Assistant Manager
International Division
(Assistant to the Chairman)

MG:mi

Appendix 15.6: Extracts from the *Sunday Times* the week prior to Dr Wills meeting with the Investment Manager of M.C. Cinti Ltd

HOME & EXPORT
AUTOMOTIVE PARTS

Remanufacturers of car and commercial clutches, steering racks, radiators and distributors of disc pads, brake shoes, clutch release bearings, & other fast-moving lines for all British models invite inquiries for home & export sales.

EXPORT
AUTOMOTIVE PARTS

Major European distributor of automotive parts invites inquiries for export sales. We hold large stocks of batteries, exhaust systems, brake pads, and shoes, shock absorbers and other fast moving parts for most European and Japanese vehicles and wish to establish trading links with companies interested in these products.

DISCUSSION POINTS

Dr Tom Wills has developed a new process to manufacture brake linings in an industry dominated by large companies.

- What are the problems associated with launching a technological breakthrough in such a market?
- What are the various possible strategies?
- How does the student evaluate the strategy proposed by Tom Wills?
- What are the factors which the merchant bank would consider when evaluating Tom Wills and his idea?

Appendix 15.7: Cash-flow Statement

	III Qtr 1976 (£)	IV Qtr 1976 (£)	I Qtr 1977 (£)	II Qtr 1977 (£)	III Qtr 1977 (£)	IV Qtr 1977 (£)	I Qtr 1978 (£)	II Qtr 1978 (£)
Manufacture:								
At sales price	32,000	40,000	48,000	50,000	55,000	60,000	60,000	60,000
At cost price	17,150	21,000	25,700	26,800	38,980	42,500	42,500	42,500
Cash from sales	6,000	21,000	40,000	50,000	50,000	50,000	55,000	65,000
Cash from grants		12,800						
Total cash in	6,000	33,800	40,000	50,000	50,000	50,000	55,000	
Value of sales	12,000	30,000	50,000	50,000	50,000	50,000	60,000	70,000
Rent	1,000	1,000	1,000	1,000	1,150	1,150	1,150	1,150
Wages: staff	1,250	1,250	1,250	1,250	2,000 (2)	2,000	2,000	2,000
operators	3,000	3,000	3,000	3,000	6,000 (3)	6,000	6,000	6,000
Services (1)	1,530	1,951	2,385	2,494	2,850	3,155	3,218	3,282
Transport (1)		312	318	325	442	457	460	469
Raw materials (1)	13,317	13,317	16,982	20,794	22,092	24,790	27,583	28,135
Miscellaneous expenses	500	500	600	600	700	700	800	800
Purchase of fixed assets	64,000							
Advertising: radio			2,000	3,000	2,000		2,000	3,000
magazines		1,500	500	500	500	1,500	500	500
Total cash out (4)	71,280	22,830	28,035	32,963	37,734	39,746	43,711	45,336
Net cash flow	(65,280)	10,970	12,965	17,037	12,266	10,254	11,289	19,664
Cash held	(62,580)	(54,310)	(42,345)	(25,308)	(13,042)	(2,788)	8,501	28,165
Positions at end period:								
Stocks at sale price	20,000	30,000	28,000	28,000	33,000	43,000	43,000	33,000
Stocks at cost price	10,720	16,080	15,000	15,000	23,390	30,470	30,470	23,390
Debtors	6,000	15,000	25,000	25,000	25,000	25,000	30,000	35,000
Creditors	13,317	16,982	20,794	22,092	24,790	27,583	28,135	28,698
Earnings after tax & interest (EATI)				19,200				39,800
EATI as % of sales				13.5				17.3

16 CAPITALISING ON DIFFERENT, BUT ASSOCIATED, PRODUCTS: COWPACT LTD*

Between 1950 and the mid 1970s, dairy-herd numbers in the UK increased from an average of 30 cows to over 80 cows. In the winter, for between 150 and 180 days, herds were usually housed indoors in cubicles or beds that were slightly shorter than the animal so that her tail could hang over the edge, raised by 9 inches from the concrete passage, and she could wander in and out at will. Every day each cow produced some 12-15 gallons of cow dung which fell into this 'loafing' area. The disposal of this slurry had become a major problem.

Confronted with this problem, Pam Murphy, herself owner/manager of a 250-acre dairy farm, with a herd of 100 pedigree Guernseys, and later 100 non-pedigree Friesians, installed a slurry separator; a machine which separated the solids from the liquid and thus made storage much easier. Much of the solid Pam sold by mail order as a garden fertiliser under the brand name 'Cowpact' (see Appendices 16.1 and 16.2). In 1978 sales had reached 25,000 bags a year.

In 1978 Pam decided to sell her farm, and concentrate on the production of Cowpact, which was more profitable than dairy farming, by using other farmer's slurry. However, the machinery she had used had suffered from corrosion and extensive usage. The manufacturers had gone out of the business of slurry separation, and there was no adequate alternative on the market. Pam had earlier had a machine fabricated but this had not been satisfactory, so she now contracted with her fabricator to build a machine that really worked, since the problems of pollution on both dairy and pig units were increasing, and other farmers were in need of such a machine for their own use. Whereas farmers would be able to sell the solids (which can be used on their own farm as organic fertiliser containing potash and phosphates), they could not use the brand-name Cowpact, and few would be likely to enter the hazards of marketing. By October 1980 the Slurrimaster had been developed and independent trials on the machine had been completed at SILSOE, the national agricultural college, with glowing results. With serious interest from both farmers and farm supply companies, Pam had to decide upon the next steps. In particular, how many machines

---

*This case was written by Sue Birley, based on material from Pam Murphy.

should she aim to sell in the first year, what arrangements should she make about Cowpact and how seriously should she pursue the development of a separator for pig slurry?

The Slurry Problem

Pam:

Slurry is very different from domestic sewage. It is not economical to treat it to produce effluent clean enough to discharge into a stream, and it has to be put on the land without causing pollution or smell nuisance, whilst making the best use of plant nutrients. The simplest way is to apply it untreated, but storage is necessary to avoid having to spread it on wet land in the winter, when crops cannot use the nutrients, and when it can often run off into ditches causing pollution.

The normal methods of disposal were:

(a) To scrape into an underground pit and then pump into a large storage tank later to be spread on the land by tanker or rain gun.
(b) To store in lagoons. Not only did these suffer from leakage, they also occupied a great deal of space and were expensive to empty since the farmer usually had to hire a JCB for the purpose.

Both of these methods had serious disadvantages for the farmer:

(a) There was high risk of pollution when slurry was spread.
(b) The land became rank and sour and for some weeks cattle would not graze where slurry had been spread.
(c) The majority of the fertiliser content was lost, since it could only be spread where land was to be ploughed, hay or silage made, or the land 'paddied', in the winter the plant cannot absorb the nutrients.
(d) Weed seeds were spread.
(e) Any disease contained in slurry (in particular brucellosis and salmonella) was spread.

The Slurrimaster

Pam:

In the early 1970s four firms produced slurry separators. None were satisfactory; they were too small, too slow and corroded fast. I had one of the first. Even so, I found that the cost benefit was great due to the better use of the nutrients in slurry and the consequent reduction in the fertiliser bill. When the firm I bought mine from went out of the separation business I had one fabricated, double the size.

When in 1978 I sold the farm, I instructed my fabricator to make me a new separator, that really worked, and with stainless steel where necessary. This has now been done and it is currently on loan to a local farmer. It separates at 1,000 gallons an hour, against 150 gallons from the old one, reducing the volume by separation into solid and liquid 50-50.

Rather than storing neat slurry until required, the Slurrimaster was able to deal with it immediately. After it had been scraped into a conventional pit it was augered or pumped into a separator hopper where it was gravity fed through a series of perforated drums and rubber rollers. The separated liquids were pumped into a storage tank ready for spraying and the solids were stacked until required. During stacking, they would compost and heat to between $170°F$ and $180°F$, thus killing pathogens and weed seeds. The benefits of this method could be summarised as follows:

1. The storage space of the liquid was doubled.
2. When the liquid was sprayed on grassland, it went straight in, and cows would graze after the first rain. Pam: 'It is invaluable in drought conditions, when granular fertiliser cannot act until after the rain.'
3. The analysis was 52N (nitrogen) 21P (phosphates) K63 (potash). At 1980 prices this was worth £22 per 1,000 gallons. Neat slurry was not a balanced fertiliser and so, by separation, proper use could be made of the nitrogen, mostly in the liquid, and the phosphates and potash, which with the trace elements were in the solids. Pam: 'From 200 cows on 250 acres I virtually eliminated the purchase of artificial compounds.'
4. Weed seeds and disease were eliminated, along with flies, which were a problem in built up areas.
5. The solids could be marketed.

6. Leaving aside tax rebates, which depended on the profitability of the dairy farm, the direct advantage was a saving of some £4,500 (1980 prices) on the fertiliser bill from the slurry from 200 cows.

Pam:

There was an increase in cost of oil or electricity of about £100 p.a. to run the machine. However, one of the greatest benefits was that separation made slurry easier to handle, and farm staff were no longer faced with the daily prospect of the disposal of vast quantities of malodorous 'porridge'.

Marketing Strategy for the Slurrimaster

In 1978, there were some 45,000 dairy farmers in the UK owning nearly 3,000,000 dairy cows, over half of which were in units of 100 or more cows. The Pollution of Rivers Act 1976 had imposed stiff penalties for pollution from slurry and many dairy farmers were in real trouble.

Pam:

I intend to order ten machines from my fabricator to be delivered between September 1980 and 1981. It is easy to find from the MMB National Milk Records the large herds within a 50-mile radius of my subcontractor. I will circularise them with details and then visit, offering to demonstrate on the farm where the prototype is operating. Extra promotion can be obtained through editorials via press releases to trade papers. I am already well known* in agricultural circles and can expect at the very least to feature in 'What's new in farming' – a free magazine to all farmers. (See Appendix 16.3.)

The fabricator proposed to charge Pam £6,500 for each machine. Added to this would be £300 for delivery, plus a charge for the first year's maintenance, plus VAT. Pam felt that a selling price of £10,000 would 'cover costs and be in line with the price of other agricultural machines':

---

*1971-7: Hon Treasurer, English Guernsey Cattle Society; 1978-80: President, English Guernsey Cattle Society; 1975-7: Chairman, National Cattle Breeders Association; 1974-80: CBI representative, Industrial Relations Tribunal.

You may well ask why it hasn't been done before. Unfortunately most of the Research Institutes lack money, personnel and resources. [See Appendix 16.4.] I have done a great deal of work with the N.I.A.E. at Silsoe, 10 miles away. When they had overseas visitors, they would bring them to my farm, with the recommendation, 'Mrs. Murphy knows more about slurry handling than any one else in the country.' Several public companies and private firms, including the NEB, have spent a lot of money on research without producing the answer. My knowledge of the problem, threats from the Anglia Water Board, and my determination to deal with it, plus a manufacturer who has dealt with tannery waste have helped to produce the answer.

By October, 1980, Pam was faced with a series of decisions:

(1) Although she had had a great deal of interest from farmers and from a large company, which owned a number of dairy herds, none had as yet been translated into orders. Should she instruct her fabricator to go ahead and manufacture, recognising that due to delay on the delivery of the rollers the manufacturing process would take at least four months? Further, how many should she order? Any increase on the forecast sales of ten machines would mean that she would have to approach the bank for funding. On the other hand, if she ordered fewer, she had a strong suspicion that the fabricator would be in severe financial difficulties, and his skills and experience would not be easily transferrable.

(2) The sale of Cowpact had ceased in 1979, but since it had been such a good source of short-term cash, Pam was considering re-launching it in 1981. She felt that her strategy of offering it only mail order was still right since shops and garden centres had storage problems and required too much mark up. There still remained, however, the question of the liquid, which Pam knew could be bottled for sale – but under what brand name? Further, what arrangement should she make for further supplies if demand exceeded the 25,000-bag capacity of the one machine on loan to a farmer friend?

(3) Late in September Pam had been telephoned by a friend who had just purchased a large pig unit from which the slurry problem was even greater than that for cows. A small amount of development work, and expenditure, on the Slurrimaster could solve the problem.

Appendix 16.1: Cowpact Advertisement

Appendix 16.2: Cowpact Advertisement

Appendix 16.3: Article in the *Sunday Times Business News* of 17 January 1975

A PAT BY ANY OTHER NAME

Pam Murphy's inspired decision to call processed manure Cow Pat – a polite but unmistakable euphemism – could make her fortune.

She realised five years ago that while the cost of keeping her 100 pedigree Guernsey cows was mounting alarmingly she had to sell their milk at fixed prices. Apart from surplus calves the only other product of her 250-acre Tyrells Manor farm at Stoke Hammond, near Milton Keynes, was the grass the cows ate. Plus a bewildering 1,300 gallons of dung for every 220 gallons of milk each day.

Four years' experiment has taught Pam Murphy the answer to cowdung's bulk and smell, the main reasons why farmyard manure is not widely used as garden fertiliser. She squeezes out most of the liquid with a giant mangle and then composts the residue for 10 days. This turns it into an easy-to-handle product with a vaguely woody smell.

When it was packed in 40lb bags and offered to local Buckinghamshire gardeners Pam Murphy was swamped with orders.

Last autumn she decided to advertise Cow Pat nationally and was astonished by the demand for "mail order muck." At £2.20 a bag delivered anywhere in Britain turnover should be at least £30,000 this year and to guarantee supplies Pam Murphy has just bought 80 Friesians. "This time I've chosen bigger cows because they produce more dung."

Appendix 16.4: Article in *Farmer's Weekly*, 30 November 1979

A pong can close intensive units

THE Department of the Environment has the power to close down intensive livestock units without compensation if action is not taken to control slurry smells.

This little-known fact was spelt out to farmers by Mr Jeff Stephenson, deputy director of environmental health with North Wolds borough council.

Ministers had been given this authority under a section of the Public Health Act, he told a conference at the Humberside College of Agriculture, Bishop Burton.

They had been lenient so far because of the high costs involved for farmers.

The department was also trying to push through a proposal which would empower local health officers to serve a notice on stock men who created a nuisance by smell.

Farmers could then find themselves in the position of having a tanker full of slurry ready for spraying and being served with a statutory notice.

"This is a warning of the way things are developing," he said.

There could be a case of a proposed housing development around an established livestock unit, and the farmer taking all

reasonable precautions, but still facing the possibility of being closed down if the local council or neighbours won a High Court action.

Consultation with environmental health officers was not mentioned within the Humberside policies for new intensive livestock units. But farmers should seek advice.

"When Ministry of Agriculture and Water Authority officials have all gone back to their offices and you are still creating a smell nuisance, the person who is going to come round and chase you up is the environment health officer," said Mr Stephenson.

Most complaints of smell nuisance came from the use of rain guns. They should be phased out, with suitable grants made available for replacement equipment.

Mr David Gill, Humberside county council's director of planning, said policies for new intensive units and expansion of existing ones were designed to provide a framework within which it was possible to strike a balance between the need to encourage efficient and viable farming and protection of the environment.

During the past five years, 356 applications for intensive livestock units had been received. Of these 266 had been approved, 48 refused and 42 were still being processed.

"Few applications are re-

jected outright," said Mr Gill. "Applicants are now aware of our policies and understand that negotiation of an acceptable solution is possible."

Managing director of the Lightwater Valley Visitors' Farm at North Stainley, Yorks, Mr Robert Staveley, told the conference: "We have to be realistic in our approach to slurry—we are being given warnings.

"Only a pathetically small amount of money is being spent on the development of satisfactory farm waste treatment systems.

"We have to press for more money to be put into research."

Mr David Stephenson, Skelfrey Park, Market Weighton, who has recently installed a treatment plant, said it was impossible to meet interest on capital and running costs of slurry treatment on the end product price.

"I had no grants," he said. "The running cost amounts to 50p to 60p on each pig sold, and I have a herd of 400 sows."

Mr Cedric Neilson, of the Ministry's farm waste disposal unit at Reading, Berks, said economic treatment of farm wastes was a world-wide problem. No one had yet come up with a satisfactory solution.

A lot of development work needed to be done on the best treatment systems for the future.

DISCUSSION POINTS

Pam Murphy has more than one potential business which she could form from the ideas and products she has developed. But some are more developed than others.

- What are the various possible ways in which Pam could capitalise on the products?
- What are the factors necessary for success in each case?
- How would the student advise Pam to choose?

17 THE BREAK-UP OF A PARTNERSHIP: STEEL FABRICATORS LTD (SFL)*

On 23 December 1978, Malcolm Evans, Managing Director of SFL, returned from a business trip to France to find a note on top of his desk. It contained the resignations of his two partners, David Cole, Sales Director, and Cyril Cox, Production Director. Further, it very soon became clear that they had decided to set up a new business in competition and by promising them a shareholding had taken a number of SFL employees with them including the company accountant, its secretary/typist, the production co-ordinator, a senior designer, a welder and a plater. Malcolm Evans had to decide whether there was any business left for him, whether he could cope with a half-completed £1.4 million contract and, indeed, whether his major investors, ICFC, would support him.

SFL was formed in 1971 by Evans, Cole and Cox to fabricate process plant in high technology metals.

Malcolm Evans:

As a qualified metallurgist and welding engineer, I had always been research oriented and had found it difficult to break out of the boffin image. However, at the age of 36 and after five years as an R & D Department Head, I finally managed to land a general management job for Bramah Process Plant Ltd, a substantial engineering company based in Sheffield. I was to replace the works manager who had left to start in competition, taking the chief designer, the assistant works manager and various tradesmen with him. I rebuilt the management structure of that company.

They both had little idea about markets and marketing and I had educated myself on the market potential by digging around in the industry. Consequently in three years, work in hand had increased from £40,000 to nearly £1,000,000 with ROI up from 1 per cent to 23 per cent on about £1,000,000 turnover (up twofold) at around 7 per cent, my salary had only gone up by 3 per cent over the period.

I had never really thought about starting on my own, although there was always talk in the company about it. But, in early 1971,

*This case was written by Sue Birley on the basis of material provided by the company, whose names have been changed.

175

serious talk developed beneath me and so I got involved, particularly as it was becoming increasingly clear to me that some private companies take advantage of you, especially when you are over 40 years of age – and I was 39. Four of us had a couple of serious discussions out of work time and then decided to shelve the idea for four or five months. However, the Managing Director found out and started a witch-hunt and after he had summarily ordered Cole back for interrogation while we were both visiting a customer, I finally quit. David Cole resigned one month later and Cyril Cox agreed to join us when we finally raised the money three months later.

With Cyril Cox's productions skills, David Cole's contacts as a sales engineer and my metallurgical background, good professional standing and general management skills, I felt we would make a strong team. However, I knew that a partnership of three people was fraught with danger, particularly as we all had very strong, aggressive personalities and so I created voting and non-voting shares so that my wife and I controlled 51 per cent of the voting shares. [See Appendix 17.1.] I wanted the last word, particularly as most of the unlimited guarantees to the bank would fall on me as the one with most assets to lose. The company was to plough back all earnings for expansion.

In June 1971, ICFC completed an investment of £15,000 in the new company. It involved a £13,500 loan and a £1,500 equity subscription in exchange for a 25 per cent holding in the business. The directors' contribution was £5,000 cash of which £2,000 was from Evans and £1,500 each from Cole and Cox. Six months later, ICFC supplied a further £5,000 working capital for an improvement in the equity holding to 28 per cent.

After this difficult start, the company began to grow and to earn reasonable profits (see Appendix 17.2) and, in 1974, ICFC felt that they had established a solid base on which to build and so provided a further loan to assist with working capital and hire purchase facilities to fund the purchase of new plant.

In 1976, the company decided to acquire a 10,000 sq. ft freehold factory in Sheffield, build an 8,800 sq. ft extension, install a new workshop with a 15-tonne crane capacity, and set up a special clean room for welding high technology metals. The workshop was later extended to 50-tonne capacity. The whole project cost £166,000 and was partly funded by ICFC and partly by retained earnings. In 1978, an adjacent 11,000 sq. ft factory was purchased, funded in full by ICFC.

By now SFL had become a major and well-regarded contractor in its specialist field, its main activity being the fabrication of corrosion resistant process plant, primarily pressure vessels and heat exchangers for the chemical industry. But this growth had not been without its internal problems so that by the end of 1977. Malcolm Evans:

There were three main areas of disagreement between David, Cyril and myself, to do with the business, our families and our remuneration. As far as the business was concerned the other two had very short horizons and did not want to continue to plough back all earnings. They believed that we should stick to what we knew about and stay small I think it was because they didn't like being account-able and I thought that we had reached the stage where more formal controls were necessary. For example, my wife and I had always done the books in our spare time but it had got too much for her and in 1976 I decided to employ a full-time accountant. In 1978 I started formal monthly management meetings. At the same time I made my wife and the chief designer, directors. I think that this made the other two finally realise that the company was not their personal property.

We never really mixed on a social level at all. Neither of them wanted his wife as a shareholder. As far as possible we kept our wives completely away from the business and out of the premises. Even my wife didn't go into the factory. We had enough complica-tions without risk of friction. Even so, resentments seemed to grow up. For example, I have two sons and one daughter and my elder son wanted to be a metallurgist like me, so I employed him in the com-pany where he labours in his vacations and sent him to Sheffield Polytechnic on a degree course. They didn't like that, but I can't see why. They only have daughters but that shouldn't stop them from similar employment in the company when of age. They could do as well. After all, someday the company shares will be theirs.

As far as remuneration was concerned, they seemed to resent the fact that I was taking more than them. Notwithstanding nearly ten years' age differences and an altogether higher earning capacity in my previous employment. But I had tried to be fair and we had agreed at the outset to use an AIC survey as a basis for setting salaries. This study showed that, on average, executive directors earned 67 per cent of the salary of the Managing Director and whilst our records show that I grossed some £19,300 in calendar year 1978 against the £15,900 each for the other two [see Appendix

17.3] , after tax I only received 11 per cent more than them – and this didn't include the Jaguars provided etc. My wife's remuneration in 1978 was £4,700.

Some of these problems had begun to surface over the previous six months, to the extent that I learnt that they had begun to deliberately undermine morale in the place. We had a chat and I insisted that we should either part on acceptable terms or stay together for at least five years. We all agreed to stay together.

When I returned from France a few days before Christmas I was devastated by their note. They had not only asked to be relieved of their responsibilities, they had also resigned as directors and left owing some £24,000 in all for house extensions which the company had paid.

Peter Folkman, ICFC:

I arranged a meeting between myself, Cole, Cox and their solicitor at which I was told that there were irreconcilable differences which appeared to stem from two sources. First they were dissatisfied with their respective remunerations and other rewards and second they were frustrated by the realisation that with 51 per cent of the votes, Evans would control the destiny of the company forever, leaving the other two vulnerable. I was concerned to persuade them to reconsider their decision, but clearly, they were adamant.

Appendix 17.1: Share Holdings

| | Authorised and issued shares | | | |
	'A' shares	%	'B' shares	%
30 September 1977				
M. Evans	1,506	50.2	564	17.4
C. Cox	372	12.4	843	25.9
D. Cole	372	12.4	843	25.9
ICFC	750	25.0	1,000	30.8
Total	3,250	100.0	3,250	100.0
30 September 1978				
M. Evans	753	25.1	564	17.4
C. Cox	372	12.4	843	25.9
D. Cole	372	12.4	843	25.9
Mrs R.P. Evans	753	25.1	1,000	30.8
P.K. Appleby	–	–	–	–
ICFC	–	25.0	–	–
Total	3,250	100.0	3,250	100.0

Appendix 17.2: Company Turnover and Profits

	Turnover	Pre-tax profit
6 months to 30 Sept. 1971	16,000	(8,000)
Year to 30 Sept. 1972	100,000	2,000
Year to 30 Sept. 1973	148,000	14,000
6 months to 31 March 1974	84,000	9,000

Appendix 17.3: Directors' Emoluments

Accounts date (year ending September)	Chairman	Other directors Range	No.
1974	£7,040	£5,001- £7,500	2
1975	£8,660	£5,991- £7,500	2
1976	£14,731	£10,001-£12,500	2
1977	£18,135	£2,501- £5,000	1
		£10,001-£12,500	2
1978	£19,331 (£10,731 take-home pay)	£5,001- £7,500	2
		£12,501-£15,000	2

Appendix 17.4: Summary and Profit and Loss Accounts, 1973-8

(£)	1973	1974	1975	1976	1977	1978
Turnover	N/A	229,400	459,441	594,684	1,210,743	1,616,104
Net trading profit	33,376	44,616	131,383	294,453	334,574	102,217
Less: Depreciation	3,674	7,457	11,245	29,530	39,194	44,803
Directors emoluments	9,788	16,160	24,955	40,704	50,150	55,685
Auditors	350	475	550	1,000	1,575	2,625
Interest on:						
Debentures	2,283	2,104	4,009	2,284	16,411	18,607
Overdraft	615	191				
Hire purchase	428	921				
Hire of equipment	2,033	1,423	2,197	2,223	3,063	4,561
	19,171	28,731	42,956	75,741	110,393	126,281
	14,025	15,885	88,427	218,712	224,181	(24,064)
Add: Interest rec'd.	—	44	1,320	8,576	31,117	12,601
Net profit before tax	14,025	15,929	89,747	227,288	193,064	(36,665)
Less: Tax	4,100	9,483	46,390 [1]	120,029	109,208	12,529
	10,105	6,446	43,357	109,784	83,856 [2]	(24,136)

Notes: 1. Plus Extraordinary Item of £2,027. 2. Plus Extraordinary Item of £12,462.

Appendix 17.5: Summary Balance Sheets 1973-8 (Year Ending September)

	1973	1974	1975	1976	1977	1978
Fixed assets	12,335	24,845	40,300	187,383	291,224	427,271
Current assets:						
Stock and WIP	9,858	20,679	104,158	274,055	521,415	168,847
Debtors	50,982	69,034	149,162	50,384	177,694	302,496
Directors loans	–	–	–	–	9,154	25,908
Short term deposits						
– bank	–	4,281	140,000	20,161	25,174	25,181
– building						
societies	–	–	–	20,000	–	20,000
Cash	90	61	13,450	25,767	141,126	191
	60,930	94,055	406,770	390,367	874,563	542,623
Less:						
Current liabilities						
Creditors	28,633	60,375	254,862	165,473	508,130	215,556
Hire purchase	3,034	4,156	13,124	27,327	–	15,833
Advance payments	–	–	35,748	18,038	25,259	46,639
Tax	–	–	5,390	11,782	–	118,071
Overdraft	10,488	–	–	–	8,667	3,800
	42,155	64,531	309,124	222,620	542,056	142,724
Net assets	31,110	54,069	137,946	355,130	623,731	569,995
Financed by:						
Share capital	6,250	6,250	6,250	6,250	6,250	6,250
Reserves	3,666	10,112	55,496	165,280	242,581	220,445
	9,916	16,362	61,746	171,530	248,831	226,695
Loans	17,094	25,007	22,500	20,000	102,500	201,500
Deferred tax	4,100	12,700	53,700	163,600	272,400	141,800
	31,110	54,069	137,946	355,130	623,731	569,995

Appendix 17.6: Fixed Assets at 30 September 1978

(£)	Cost	Depreciation	Net book value
Leasehold property	2,000	–	–
Plant and machinery	175,231	101,333	73,898
Fixtures and fittings	14,376	4,005	10,371
Furniture and equipment	31,172	7,808	23,364
Motor vehicles	14,998	5,337	9,661
Freehold property	313,344	5,367	307,977

Appendix 17.7: Loans (Year Ending September)

	1974	1975	1976	1977	1978
14¾% debenture repayable by 10 fixed annual instalments of £2,500 (secured)	25,000 [1]	22,500	20,000	17,500	15,000
16½% debenture repayable by 10 fixed annual instalments of £8,500 (secured)				85,000	76,500
13¾% debenture repayable by 17 half yearly instalments of £6,100					110,000
	25,000	22,500	20,000	102,500	201,500

Note: 1. Initial loan of £16,500 renegotiated with ICFC.

DISCUSSION POINTS

This case picks up the partnership problems hinted at in Light Engineering. History has repeated itself and Malcolm Evans' two partners have left to start again on their own.

- In what way does SFL become a new business?
- Does Malcolm Evans have any options other than to continue?
- What actions does he have to take in the immediate future?
- What factors should Peter Folkman take into account when deciding how to advise Malcolm Evans?
- What price should Malcolm Evans pay to buy out his partners?

Case A

Late in March 1975, Bob Kent and Patrick Thorpe were ushered into Robert Smith's office, in the Brighton branch of ICFC. In February they had made an application for a loan in order to purchase Certikin Ltd, the company which they managed, from its owner and this was to be the meeting when they would hear whether their application had been favourably received.

Bob Kent:
It was a sunny day and I had just bought some new tinted-down spectacles which had automatically darkened. I was obviously concerned that I looked like a member of the Mafia and so I spent 15 minutes riding up and down in the lift waiting for them to lighten. Then Robert Smith sat me in the sun!

Certikin was started in 1965 by Brian Stannah, son of Leslie Stannah who owned Stannah Lifts, to manufacture and market swimming pool accessories.

Bob Kent:
At the time I was 19, working as an estimator in a large construction company, when Brian Stannah, a family friend, asked me if I would like to join him in a new venture. I couldn't see what I had to lose — I had always wanted to be a manager.

Our first financial year was terrible. For example, in January 1966, with a monthly break-even of £400, we billed £96. Nevertheless, it was exciting. I remember that our first order was for £126 to supply a diving board and chlorine equipment, when I left the client I was in such a daze that I went straight home and took the rest of the day off!

In 1967, with an average day starting at 6.00 a.m. and finishing around 9.00 p.m., we finally took off. We had managed to develop a nice niche in the market by designing products and packaging them

*This case was written by Sue Birley.

and marketing them imaginatively. It wasn't so difficult, as most of our competitors came from the 'gin and watercress sandwich, back from the pub at 3.00 p.m.' lot. They were very nice people but constrained – and we weren't.

From its inception, Bob Kent had been responsible for all aspects of the business, from design through to marketing, with Brian Stannah acting as non-executive chairman. Throughout its growth, all the books had been written up each week by the auditors but by 1972 with an annual turnover of £100,000 and 14 employees, it was clear that a full-time accountant was necessary. After interviewing a number of candidates, Brian Stannah and Bob Kent finally appointed Patrick Thorpe. Patrick, who was 22 at the time, had worked for three companies whilst studying for his accountancy qualifications. His first job, which lasted just over three years, was with the Petbow; then he had a brief spell at ITT where he felt that there was 'too much competition', and finally he was the accountant for Heinz-Erin Foods, a small marketing company in the Heinz group. When it became clear that he was to be moved back to Head Office, where he would become 'a small fish again', he began to look around for a smaller company. Certikin was perfect.

Patrick Thorpe:
Bob Kent offered me less than the advertised salary because he said I was very young. Still I took the job because it was clear that there was plenty of opportunity for me. Certikin was basically a good business. It was very cash rich but no-one either used or even controlled it! Everyone was more concerned with getting stuff out of the door, and in their current premises even this was a problem. The company was literally bursting at the seams.

In 1973, two major strategic decisions were taken. First, it was decided to move from the existing, overcrowded premises in East Grinstead to new, larger ones in Oxted; and second a major new marketing initiative in Germany was started.

Bob Kent:
On reflection, we managed it badly. There had been a very friendly atmosphere in the old premises and people had worked hard. In fact, we never really knew how many we had in the place. For example, Rose, one of the assemblers, had eight kids and they used to come into the factory after school and lend a hand assembling, which

obviously gave us a false impression of what one person could do. When we moved, we took our time and used a lot of small lorries, but we didn't involve the staff. Because of this we had a lot of settling-in problems. People started to set up territories and demarkation lines. As a result, efficiency dropped by 30 per cent.

Added to all this, our old 5,000-square-foot premises had cost us 2s 6d per square foot, but we were able to offset most of this by sub-letting some adjoining garages. Our new premises would cost us £12,000 per year.

Patrick Thorpe:
The German venture was a disaster. It involved numerous trips over there to set up the company and make all the necessary contacts. Both Bob and I were against it but Brian wanted to do it. Mind you, there was great potential, but we felt the company wasn't ready – we just hadn't enough people to cope.

Patrick estimated that by early 1974 a total of £130,000 had been invested in the German venture but with the oil crisis upon them there was no immediate prospect of any significant returns. To compound the problem, the UK market for bolt-on accessories suddenly collapsed and Certikin was forced to look at other export markets. December 1974 saw the company with a turnover for the month of £1,000 and with 28 employees occupying 18,000 square feet.

Bob Kent:
I became very depressed and apathetic. I could see everything that I had worked for over the past eight years going down the pan. Brian Stannah was alright. It was in real terms a part-time activity for him. Still, he had made me Managing Director and I'm no quitter. I hate failure so we all decided to get our heads down and try to work through it.

Earlier in 1974, Certikin had been visited by a Canadian company – Convertible Pool Products International – who were so impressed with what they saw that they made a bid to acquire the company to use as their UK warehousing and sales operation.[1] The offer came at an opportune time for Brian Stannah. At the time his family was requesting

---

1. By this time only a small amount of final assembly was handled by Certikin, almost all manufacture being subcontracted mainly to injection moulders.

for more of his time and for his Bank Guarantees to be brought in-house, as Stannah Lift Services had decided to purchase free-hold property in Andover from where they would increase their manufacture and distribution of a new range of lift apparatus in the UK and over-seas. By February 1975 negotiations were almost complete.

Bob Kent:
We were so busy working, trying to negotiate and survive at the time that we had no time to think about being an owner. I had got to the point where I was falling asleep in restaurants and my wife was pressurising me to leave. It was merely by chance that Russell, our Auditor, said why didn't we buy it ourselves? That night I went to see Brian Stannah and asked if he would sell it to me if I could put up the same money as the Canadians.[2] He said he would stall them for ten days for me to see if I could raise the finance. I decided to talk to Patrick and to our sales director. Patrick had just seen an ICFC advertisement in the paper and so immediately followed it up and got in touch with Robert Smith.

There were three issues which the partners were concerned with. First there was the long term viability of the business; second there was the effect on their personal lives; and third there was their future management style.[3]

Bob Kent:
For our money we would be getting a network of dealers, an internationally-known trademark and some undervalued tooling. [See Appendix 18.1 for market data.] So we were buying potential. Mind you, it would give us a chance to try out all our new ideas. Brian Stannah had always been very conservative — he would never let you 'do a deal'. For example, I was convinced that we could make a great deal more money if we scrapped all our assembly work and subcontracted it.

Patrick Thorpe:
We had never seen each other socially and yet we were considering a long-term partnership. Nevertheless, it felt right. Bob and I think

2. Brian Stannah wished to take out his £25,000 loan and sever connections with the company.
3. Appendices 18.2-18.6 show management and statutory accounts available at the time.

alike. Our Sales Director, who was asked if he would like to become involved, somehow seemed to get left behind. He wanted everything to be too formal and that wasn't our style. Our wives also had to be behind us and mine was very concerned that it may go wrong and muck up my future career possibilities.

Bob Kent:
Those ten days were like a 100 per cent dream. Nothing really worried me. It was just a matter of putting our heads down and getting the best deal. I knew that I could market the products and Patrick would keep us on a tight financial rein. Together, and with a sense of humour, I was sure we could manage it. Right in the middle of the negotiations, I learnt that a French customer was going broke – he owed us £21,000 ECGD covered and we needed their money now.

Patrick Thorpe:
Brian Stannah had always done bank negotiations as guarantor and this was the only thing which worried me as I sat in Robert Smith's office.

Appendix 18.1: Market Data

Certikin Ltd was engaged in the design, manufacture and marketing of 'bolt-on accessories' for swimming pools including filters, skimmers, underwater lighting, diving boards and shutes. The UK market was around £6,000,000, demand being met by a large number of small companies.

The market leaders in 1975 were Certikin, Norcal, Capital Pools, Swimquip and Aquatech, each with sales of around £200,000 per annum. Most sold US-manufactured goods, Certikin being the largest supplier of UK-manufactured goods. The goods were distributed through swimming pool construction companies or retail agents.

Appendix 18.2: Summary of Trading Results

(£)	Year ending 30 April				
	1970	1971	1972	1973	1974
Sales	73,000	106,000	185,000	308,000	391,000
Gross profit	18,100	26,100	67,700	91,400	105,500
Directors remuneration	5,400	5,800	12,100	14,600	17,100
Interest	400	1,100	1,400	2,000	3,300
Depreciation	2,900	2,000	6,500	14,900	12,600
Net profit before tax	(1,400)	(3,200)	12,200	6,600	(26,300)
Tax	–	–	1,400	3,000	(3,000)
Profit retainer	(1,400)	(3,200)	10,800	3,600	(23,300)
Profits shown in management accounts[1]	N/A	10,600	29,100	42,300	3,700 [2]

Notes: 1. Excludes an £8,000 management fee paid to Brian Stannah. 2. In the opinion of the company financial advisers, the true value of the stock at 30 April 1974 was £60,000 and not £25,000, as shown in the filed accounts. The effect of this adjustment is to increase the net profits by some £35,000.

Appendix 18.3: Trading Profit and Loss Account (as per Management Accounts)

£	Actual May 1974 – Nov. 1974	Actual May 1974 – Jan. 1975	May 1974 – April 1975	Budgeted May 1975 – April
Sales	186,005	199,548	296,000	350,000
Less Cost of Sales				
Stock 1st May	75,258	75,258	75,258	68,000
Purchases	115,051	119,639	160,000	218,500
Loose Tools	–	–	–	500
	190,309	194,897	235,000	287,000
Less Stock at Year end	82,806	80,408	62,000	67,000
	107,503	114,489	173,000	220,000
Wages	5,201	6,112	7,200	6,000
Carriage/Packing	2,818	3,829	4,500	1,500
	115,522	124,430	184,700	227,500
Gross Profit	70,483	75,118	111,300	122,500

Appendix 18.3: (continued)

£	Actual		Budgeted	
	May 1974 – Nov. 1974	May 1974 – Jan. 1975	May 1974 – April 1975	May 1975 – April
Less Administration				
Salaries/Pensions	17,892	22,356	30,500	23,000
Rent/Rates	9,974	12,974	17,300	11,000
Light/Heat	299	532	800	1,500
Insurance	2,728	3,507	4,600	3,000
Telephone/Telex	2,365	2,967	4,000	4,500
Bank Charges	1,939	3,083	4,500	6,000
Travel/Motor	5,341	6,536	8,500	10,000
Printing/Stationery	1,469	1,712	3,000	2,000
Advertising	3,407	4,219	6,000	4,500
Bad Debts	470	470	–	–
Petty Cash	1,832	2,377	3,300	–
Postage	769	869	1,300	2,000
Miscellaneous	1,004	1,168	1,800	6,000
	49,489	62,770	86,000	73,500
	20,994	12,348	25,300	49,000
Less HP Interest	1,551	1,908	2,800	2,500
Audit Fees	–	150	750	1,000
Depreciation	6,906	9,126	12,000	10,500
Directors Fees	11,211	14,583	19,250	13,000
	19,668	25,767	34,800	27,000
Net Profit (Loss)	1,326	(13,419)	(9,500)	22,000
Profit from sale of lease:				12,000
Cash flow improvement:				34,000

Appendix 18.4: Balance Sheets – Management Accounts

£	30 Nov. 1974		31 Jan. 1975		30 April 1975		30 April 1976	
Fixed assets³								
Plant and equipment	47,278		49,293		50,000		50,000	
Less depreciation	34,421	12,857	35,995	13,298	38,200	11,800	46,000	4,000
Motor vehicles	15,625		14,183		15,000		15,000	
Less depreciation	5,460	9,805	5,555	8,628	7,000	8,000	9,000	6,000
Office equipment	4,875		4,875		5,000		5,000	
Less depreciation	1,225	3,650	1,285	3,590	1,700	3,300	2,500	2,500
		26,312		25,516		23,100		12,500
Investment in German subsid.		8,053		8,053		–		–
Current assets								
Debtors	83,150		72,561		90,000		82,000	
Certikin Gmbh	7,893		7,893		6,000		–	
Stock	82,806		80,408		62,000		67,000	
Cash	15	173,864	15	160,877	–	158,000	–	149,000
Total assets		208,229		194,446		181,100		161,500
Less current liabilities								
Creditors	65,862		64,044		46,100		45,000	
HP accounts	14,448		12,106		13,000		4,000	
Overdraft²	33,501	113,811	38,625	114,775	35,000	94,100	18,000	67,000
		94,418		79,671		87,000		94,500
Represented by								
Share capital	10,000¹		10,000		100		100	
Long-term loan A/C	–		–		25,000		25,000	
Revenue reserve	84,418	94,418	69,671	79,671	61,900	87,000	69,400	94,500

Notes to Appendix 18.4: 1. A notional amount. The statutory accounts showed share capital of £100, 95 per cent owned by Mr Stannah and 5 per cent by Mr Kent, and a £30,000 loan due to Mr Stannah. 2. The overdraft facility was increased to £40,000 in October 1974, guaranteed by Mr Stannah, and with the bank taking a first floating charge over all the assets. 3. As at April 1974, subcontractors held Certikin moulds and tools with a combined value of £65,000. These had all been written off for balance sheet purposes.

Appendix 18.5: Balance Sheets — Statutory Accounts

£	30 April 1974		31 Jan. 1975	
Fixed assets				
Plant and equipment	47,600		49,293	
Less depreciation	29,100	18,500	35,995	13,298
Motor vehicles	16,200		14,183	
Less depreciation	6,200	10,000	5,555	8,628
Office equipment	4,500		4,875	
Less depreciation	1,000	3,500	1,285	3,590
		32,000		25,516
Investment in Certikin GmbH				
Current assets				
Debtors	123,400		56,927	
Certikin Gmbh	6,900		6,000	
Stock	25,100		80,408	
Cash	–		15	
		155,400		143,350
Total assets		187,400		168,866
Less current liabilities				
Creditors[1]	139,400		93,444	
HP accounts	20,600		14,105	
Tax	1,400		–	
Overdraft	8,600		38,625	
		170,000		146,174
		17,400		22,692
Represented by				
Share capital		100		100
Loan account: Mr Stannah		30,000		30,000
Revenue reserve		(12,700)		(7,408)

Note: 1. Includes £30,000 management fee due to a partnership under the control of the major shareholder.

Appendix 18.6: Budgeted Cash Flow, Financial Year 1976

£'000	Apr.	May	June	July	Aug.	Sept.	Oct.	Nov.	Dec.	Jan.	Feb.	Mar.	Apr.
Opening balance	(43)	(46)	(42)	(36)	(29)	(29)	(27)	(23)	(16)	(15)	(13)	(14)	(19)
Income													
Collections	27	20	30	35	30	35	32	28	24	21	18	22	26
Other		14											
Total	27	34	30	35	30	35	32	28	24	21	18	22	26
Balance	(16)	(12)	(12)	(1)	(1)	(6)	(5)	(5)	(8)	(6)	(5)	(8)	(7)
Outgoings													
Fixed O/H	10	6	10	6	6	10	7	6	10	6	7	10	6
Purchases	19	24	12	21	24	23	20	15	13	12	12	17	19
Others incl. BLRS	1	–	2	1	–	–	1	–	–	1	–	–	–
Total	30	30	24	28	30	33	28	21	23	19	19	27	25
Closing	(46)	(42)	(36)	(29)	(29)	(27)	(23)	(16)	(15)	(13)	(14)	(19)	(18)

DISCUSSION POINTS

Case A — One method by which old businesses are saved, and thus new businesses are born, is by the process of a management|buy-out. Bob Kent and Patrick Thorpe want to raise money to buy the business which they manage from its owner.

- In what ways could ownership affect their lives?
- What factors should Robert Smith take into account before arriving at a decision?
- What, if any, further information might Robert Smith need?

Case B

Well lads, if all that you tell me is true, you've got your money.

It simply remained for Robert Smith to satisfy himself that the proposition which Bob Kent and Patrick Thorpe had put forward was a viable one.

Robert Smith:
I immediately made arrangements to visit the factory. You can always get a better idea of people on their own ground: and what I saw, I liked. There was obviously a strong rapport between the partners and the work-force.

As far as the partners themselves were concerned, they seemed to be very well matched. The emphasis of the company had to be on marketing, and Bob Kent is a born salesman and entrepreneur with plenty of drive and energy. Patrick Thorpe complements this by being studious, well informed and interested in detail. Indeed, the production and stock-control systems were impressive for such a small company and, although there was room for improvement on costing records, Patrick Thorpe, an ACMA [Association of Cost and Management Accountant], was aware of this and considered that he had already achieved much in his two years with the company.

As a result of Robert Smith's investigations, a deal was finally struck. During the subsequent year, the company was very successful – achieving all the expectations of the two partners.

Bob Kent:
You come in Monday morning to the same office and say 'that's my desk' – though the drawer belongs to ICFC. Mind you, I couldn't complain. ICFC stayed away and didn't interfere – much to my surprise. But I didn't really like the deal we made. It seemed to me that they were just like another absentee landlord, taking advantage of our success without doing anything. For every £100 we made, £30 was theirs. It was just too much.

In September 1976, just twelve months after signing the original deal, Bob Kent and Patrick Thorpe visited Robert Smith again: 'We want you to reduce your holding to 20 per cent by selling us 10 per cent of your shares.'

Appendix 18.7: Trading Profit and Loss Account – Year Ending 30 April 1976

	1976		1975	
	(£)	(£)	(£)	(£)
Sales		380,875		289,511
Cost of sales				
Stock at 1 May 1975	39,787		25,086	
Purchases	264,888		168,628	
Loose tools	834		24	
	305,509		193,738	
Less: Stock at 30 April 1976	63,236		39,787	
	242,273		153,951	
Wages	5,242		14,079	
Carriage and packing	2,926	250,441	4,521	172,551
Gross profit for the year		130,434		116,960
Administration and overheads				
Directors' remuneration	18,544		11,435	
Salaries	28,197		22,190	
Sales and commission	1,795		–	
Rent and rates	11,391		17,994	
Light and heat	1,115		755	
Insurance	2,946		4,328	
Telephone	3,224		3,676	
Bank charges	7,615		4,786	
Travelling expenses	15,635		11,333	
Printing and stationery	2,883		2,262	
Postage	1,542		1,229	
Advertising	2,560		4,184	
Legal and professional	2,487		4,268	
Bad debts	2,327		3,498	
Sundry expenses	2,707		695	
Repairs and renewals	306		385	
Telex	918		659	
Experimental	459		671	
Hire purchase charges	1,803		2,694	
Audit and accountancy	1,432		1,425	
Depreciation	9,494		11,703	
		120,380		110,170
Trading profit for the year		£10,054		£6,790

Appendix 18.8: Balance Sheet 30 April 1976

	Notes	1976 (£)	1976 (£)	1975 (£)	1975 (£)
Fixed assets	3		51,734		23,907
Investment in subsidiary	8		1		1
			51,735		23,908
Current assets					
Stock	1	63,236		39,787	
Amount due from					
subsidiary co.		7,731		7,893	
Debtors		122,157		84,661	
Cash in hand		15		115	
		193,139		132,456	
Current liabilities					
Amounts due under hire					
purchase agreements		7,404		11,629	
Creditors		160,047		100,509	
Bank overdraft (secured)		12,549		42,641	
		180,000		154,779	
Net current assets (liabilities)			13,139		(22,323)
			£64,874		£1,585
Financed by:					
Share capital	9		10,143		100
Reserves	10		12,094		1,485
			22,237		1,585
Debenture	11		15,000		–
Deferred taxation	1		27,637		–
			£64,874		£1,585

Appendix 18.9: Notes to the Accounts – for the year ended 30 April 1976

1. Accounting Policies

 a. Turnover

 Turnover represents the invoiced value of sales during the year after deducting returns and allowances.

 b. Stock

 Stock quantities are ascertained by actual count and are valued at the lower of cost and net realisable value.

 c. Depreciation

 Depreciation is provided at rates calculated to write off the cost of fixed assets over the period of their estimated useful working lives.

d. Deferred Taxation

Provision is made under the Liability method for deferred taxation arising from stock relief and the excess of tax allowances on Fixed Assets over the corresponding depreciation charged in the Accounts.

2. Directors' Emoluments

	1976	1975
The emoluments of the Chairman for the year were:	11,432	1,115

The number of directors excluding the above whose emoluments fell within the following ranges were:

	1976	1975
£ Nil – £2,500	1	1
£2,501 – £5,000	1	1

3. Fixed Assets

	Short leasehold property	Fixtures and fittings	Plant and machinery	Motor vehicles	Total
Cost					
Balance at 1 May 1975	–	4,875	50,635	13,121	68,631
Additions in year	3,003	700	3,130	4,075	10,008
	3,003	5,575	53,765	17,196	79,539
Less: Disposals	–	2,925	–	–	2,925
Balance at 30 April 1976	£3,003	£2,650	£53,765	£17,196	£76,614
Depreciation					
Balance at 1 May 1975	–	1,375	38,093	5,256	44,724
Amounts written back	–	–	28,213	–	28,213
	–	1,375	9,880	5,256	16,511
Eliminated on disposals	–	1,125	–	–	1,125
	–	250	9,880	5,256	15,386
Charge for the year	–	715	6,811	1,968	9,494
	–	£965	£16,691	£7,224	£24,880
Net Book Value					
At 30 April 1976	£3,003	£1,685	£37,074	£9,972	£51,734
At 30 April 1975	–	£3,500	£12,542	£7,865	£23,907

4. Taxation

	1976	1975
Over-provision in previous years	–	(3,150)
Transfer to Deferred Taxation	5,370	–
	£5,370	£(3,150)

There is no liability to UK Corporation Tax arising from the trading activities of the Company for the year.

5. Extraordinary Items

Extraordinary Items represents profits, less losses, on the disposal of fixed assets during the year; after making a charge of £3,500 to Deferred Taxation.

6. Prior Year Adjustments

Over-provision for depreciation in previous years written back	28,213
Less: Transfer to Deferred Taxation (see Note 1)	18,767
	£9,446

7. Appropriations

Capitalisation arising from bonus issue of Preference shares	10,000
Transfer to Debenture Redemption Reserve Fund	1,500
	£11,500

8. Investment in Subsidiary

The Company owns the whole of the share capital of Certikin Gmbh, a company incorporated in West Germany. Accounts are not consolidated as, in the Directors' opinion, this would be misleading.

9. Share Capital

	(£)
Ordinary Shares of £1 each	100
Cumulative Convertible Participating Preferred Ordinary Shares of £1 each	43
7 per cent Non-cumulative Preference Shares of £1 each	10,000
	10,143

10. *Reserves*

	(£)
Profit and Loss Account	10,594
Debenture Redemption Reserve Fund	1,500
	12,094

11. *Debenture*

18½ per cent Debenture, repayable over five years by equal half-yearly instalments.

12. *Contingent Liabilities*

There is a contingent liability in respect of various banking transactions amounting to £15,850.

DISCUSSION POINTS

Case B – Put yourselves in the shoes of Robert Smith
- How would you evaluate Certikin's performance since your investment?
- What factors would you take into account when considering Bob and Patrick's request?
- How would you value your shareholding?

19 TRANSLATING THE DREAM INTO A BUSINESS

This book has attempted to demonstrate that businesses are not suddenly born, but rather that they evolve and emerge through a combination of circumstances, some luck and some pre-planned. Whilst a number of the difficulties which the entrepreneur faces will be of his own making, a function of his own personality, many will be inherent in the type of business he is proposing. For example, manufacturing businesses like Eurobond Laminates which need plant and equipment, and thus money, present different problems from Girogift, the service business which has no credibility. Whichever is the case, however, a point in time will arise when the owner has to choose whether to move from operating in the black economy, through the grey to the white; whether to translate a self-employment activity into a fully fledged business, or whether, as in the case of Certikin, an existing business can grow and so support new owners. At such a point it is important that all aspects of the business are fully considered so that, as far as possible, the balance between luck and judgement is controlled. Indeed, in some cases, the preparation of a formal business plan is a prerequisite of any negotiation for investment capital. This chapter discusses, with the entrepreneur, the questions which he should be considering and, whilst it focuses particularly upon the content and presentation of a written document, the questions and issues raised are relevant to anyone trying to translate the dream of Alan Sealey and Seamach, through the plans of Colin Goss and PEI to the reality for Malcolm Evans and Steel Fabricators.

The Business Plan

Your business plan is an opportunity to convince both yourself and any potential investors that the project you are proposing is viable. Therefore you should view it not only as a proposal to be used for raising capital but also as a strategic plan for the business, to be used to monitor and control future performance. It is possible, therefore, that it will be substantial and, perhaps, complex. However, your investors will not have the advantage of your familiarity with the product or market and so it is important to ensure that the document is RELEVANT/

LEGIBLE/EASY TO FOLLOW and COMPREHENSIVE. The latter point implies that you must include data or information on all aspects of the proposed business, organised in a logical fashion, and covering:

a description of the:	PRODUCT
	TECHNOLOGY
	MARKET
	COMPETITION
your proposed:	MARKET STRATEGY
	PRODUCT STRATEGY
	ORGANISATION STRATEGY
which you expect to result in:	MONEY TO BE INVESTED
	FORECAST CASH FLOWS
	FORECAST PROFITS

In order to help your reader digest such a wealth of information it is essential that your document should start with a SUMMARY. Not only will this help him to organise his thoughts and understand the size and nature of the proposed project, but it can also serve to arrest and capture his interest. It must be remembered that investors deal with many applications each day and a badly presented proposal can at best irritate and antagonise and at worst totally mislead. Your summary must persuade him to continue to read the rest of the document because your product is interesting, the project may be viable and you seem to know what you are doing. It should cover, ideally, one page but certainly no more than two and explain:

(a) What is the product:	a short description highlighting the special features.
(b) Who you are:	introduce yourself and show any special expertise which will give the investor confidence that you are likely to be successful.
(c) What you want:	the magnitude of the project, giving some idea of the amounts of money involved and the proportion of external funding you are seeking.
(d) What you want it for:	whether it is in the main for capital investment, further research and

	development or for working capital.
(e) The state of play:	how far you have progressed in setting up your company – whether you have registered patents, negotiated premises etc.
(f) The likely returns:	the expected rates of return and the time scales involved.

The Product or Service

The product or service which you are proposing to offer is the basis of the proposed business. Therefore, it is essential that you give a clear explanation both of WHAT IT IS and WHAT IT IS INTENDED TO BE USED FOR. Where possible you should illustrate the proposal with diagrams or samples. This is particularly important where the product is complex and your reader cannot automatically be assumed to appreciate it immediately. Your explanation should take account, therefore, of the likely level of understanding of the reader. Any technical explanations, which are essential to the complete evaluation of the product, should be reserved for the appendix. This will allow your reader to obtain technical advice reasonably easily.

A description of the product should lead straight to an explanation of WHAT IS SPECIAL ABOUT IT. In marketing terms, its UNIQUE SELLING PROPOSITION or USP. ME TOO products, or direct copies of existing products, are unattractive to potential investors, particularly when, as is often the case, the competing products are produced by larger, more experienced companies with market MUSCLE and branded products.

Nevertheless, you must recognise that there are very few new products or ideas, just variations on old ones. Continental Trucking, PEI and N & Z Hi-fi are proposing to offer a better service than competitors. John Pyke, Rod Senior and Malise Graham have all taken an existing idea and translated it into a new market. Pam Murphy has taken advantage of a changing environment to redesign a product previously marketed. Even David Jones, with his Omniclock, has designed a variation on a very old-established theme. Some of these proposed businesses need new capital, some do not, but to survive the first few months and to establish the business in the long term, both you and they need to take a long hard look at competition and be sure of what is SPECIAL. So, for example, can it:

- do a more effective job,
- do more tasks,
- be faster,
- look better,
- be smaller,
- require less skill to handle?

Whatever the level of technical sophistication involved in the product, the possibility of it being copied arises. Indeed, this is a very real worry for many entrepreneurs. There are, however, various ways of protecting yourself, the most commonly known being the registration of either a patent or copyright. In law these are, indeed, protection, but in reality the cost of litigation, both in terms of time and money, can itself destroy the business. The most effective protection for the new business must be the business itself and its credibility in the market place. But how to get there? It is here that you must seriously consider how best to capitalise on your idea. Think for a moment about the services of Lingua Franca and Girogift, and the product Cowpact. Credibility, and thus strength, has been established in the choice of name and, as such, they have a strong chance of becoming generic terms. In this way, any future competition can only help to market their products.

Not all products or ideas necessarily form the basis of a new business, some would sit much more comfortably within a larger, already-established business. The growing-bag container requires the balance of other counter-seasonal products. The new process suggested by Tom Wills could greatly threaten all the large brake lining manufacturers – or help one of them. Pam Murphy's Slurrimaster requires large capital sums, technical support and a marketing network, all of which the large farm machinery manufacturers already have. In all these cases, selling or licensing your product could establish it in the market place more efficiently and faster than you could, and at the same time make you more money. 'But what would I do then?' is your question. Recognise your own skills, which may be to translate ideas into products rather than products into businesses – you might be well advised to be in the business of selling yourself!

Whatever you decide, in the preparation of your plan, you must be clear about any problems you are encountering and how you think they will be overcome. Even if your potential investor eventually decides to reject your propositions he may be able to give you some advice or help in dealing with, for example, technical or legal issues.

The Technology

The technology and the product may go hand in hand. Indeed, like RES or Eurobond Laminates, your PRODUCT may be a new TECHNO-LOGICAL PROCESS. In such cases this section merges with the previous one. If that is not the case then, where appropriate, outline the ESSENTIAL FEATURES of the technology and process you intend to use. Indeed, recognise that, like both Pam Murphy and Tom Wills, you may have both a new process and a resultant new product. Keep in mind always that your reader is not an inventor, nor is he necessarily technically competent. However, he does prefer to be armed with the facts rather than fed selected snippets, a strategy which can sometimes suggest that the inventor is deliberately hiding possible major future snags. It is also useful, if appropriate, to include a note on any independent assessments of the product or process. Remember how the report from SILSOE reinforced your view of the credibility of the Slurrimaster.

One important way of convincing your reader of your COMPETENCE is to outline the technical RISKS and PROBLEMS, both within and outside your control, and to show how you intend to try to MINIMISE the RISK and PRE-EMPT the PROBLEMS. Indeed, this applies to all aspects of the business. Remember how Richard Brown's description of the need to consider bribery convinced you that he understood his market, even if you disapproved. Beware, however, that you do not fall into the trap of becoming a PERPETUAL INVENTOR, refining your product to such an extent that it almost develops into a universal panacea. Usually the most successful businesses are built on the simplest products or ideas.

If you are dealing with a new product, you must show whether you have progressed beyond producing one or two PROTOTYPES. If you have developed a new process, has it been tested beyond the LABORA-TORY or WORK BENCH? Remember that snags which you can deal with personally often assume enormous proportions when extended to a factory or workshop or to a production plant. Your reader must know how far you have got in testing the PRODUCTION FEASIBILITY.

It is possible that at this stage a description of your PRODUCTION STRATEGY follows naturally. If that is so remember that your reader will need some idea of its magnitude as measured, for example, by forecast annual sales. Only in that way, is he able to evaluate your proposed production capacity.

The Market

The market that you are aiming for must be both DESCRIBED AND QUANTIFIED. From this your investor will determine how you have FOCUSED your efforts and how REALISTIC you have been. For example, a proposal which includes a major worldwide launch of a new type of writing implement would be unfocused, and an attempt to snatch 90 per cent of an already-established market from an already-established company could well be unrealistic.

Therefore, first of all your proposal should describe from the customer view:

1. The total market, both geographically and by customer needs, as in The Box or RES.
2. How you see the market currently being segmented, as Robert Barclay has for Lingua Franca.
3. The size of the segment you are aiming for, as Rod Senior has attempted in Girogift.

Customer segments are often built up òn the basis of external, measurable variables such as age, socio-economic income group, or location, but these are only valid if the segments defined reflect identifiable differences in purchasing behaviour. It is worth reflecting whether Mr Singh has truly understood the difference in purchasing habits between a market customer and a shop customer – even if they are the same person.

Remember, also, that the required amount and accuracy of the data should be a function of both the availability of such data and the market share you expect to attain. Consequently, if you are aiming for a very small share of a large segment, data need not be as accurate as if you are aiming to penetrate, say, 30 per cent of the segment within a short period of time.

You must also distinguish between potential market and your ability, or even need to satisfy the whole of that market. In other words, is your strategy to be supply led or market led? Pam Murphy intends to sell ten machines in order to 'test-market' the product and her decision is crucial to her capital needs. Robert Barclay has some flexibility on the number of courses he offers but he is initially constrained by the availability of the space in University College.

Secondly, you must show some clear understanding of your proposed customers, their needs and preferences. It may be that this has already been covered, in part, in your description of the product itself. Nevertheless, such an analysis can lead easily into the third important aspect of the market: COMPETITION. This section should also divide into two. First, there are the major products with which you are intending to compete, their price, quality and suitability for the job; and secondly, the companies manufacturing those products. Both for the products and the companies you will need to be able to explain:

– how many there are
– whether they are large or small
– how strong they are

in order to arrive at some conclusion as to the effect that your proposed entry is likely to have and, consequent upon that, whether they are likely to react and in what way.

Whilst this may all seem somewhat heavy-handed, particularly in markets such as the ones which Light Engineering is proposing to approach where the potential could be seen as limitless, it is an important further step in identifying clearly what you are selling, and to whom. Further, it enables you to be more secure in your decision about your initial size. Successfully running any business depends upon the ability to balance supply and demand. In the start-up phase this is even more crucial. So, for example, is Mike Ford proposing to start with too great a capacity in his factory? Is the range offered by N & Z Hi-fi too great for them to handle, and too sophisticated for their customer needs? Is there significant gap in the market for yet another language school? We do not know the answers to any of these questions before the event – there is no substitute for actual orders. Nevertheless, a cold, hard look at the market should reduce some of the risks.

Market Strategy

Having outlined the market you are aiming for, you are now in a position to explain exactly how you intend to attack the market – what is your proposed marketing strategy? Remember that marketing is not merely selling, but a number of activities and decisions aimed at making your potential customers both aware of your product and in a position to be able to buy it. These decisions are summarised in the MARKETING MIX:

PRICE,
PROMOTION,
PRODUCT and
PLACE.

1. Price

It is very important to make sure that the price you have chosen fits both the market place and the output you expect to achieve. In finally choosing a price it is advisable to err on the high rather than on the low side. Once you have launched a new product, it is often more difficult to adjust your prices by raising them than by lowering them. Too low a price at unexpectedly low volumes can mean disaster. A higher price with generous margins will leave more room for error and thus buy time.

The price you finally choose will probably take into account all attributable costs plus some element of profit. This is known as COST-PLUS pricing. This is a useful way of estimating the price at which you need to sell your product, at the expected volumes, in order to reach some profit goal. However, you must make sure that all costs are included. One mistake which many entrepreneurs make when costing products is to exclude the cost of their own time – or rather not to fully cost it. This, of course, is why many fringe craft markets survive and why many self-employed operators are able to undercut established businesses, and as long as you do not intend to expand and to employ others, this is a personal choice which you are entitled to make.

Whilst cost-plus pricing is necessary, it is not sufficient since it does not take account of customer or competitive reaction. So, for example, if you are intending to sell your product at a premium price, you must be able to show good MARKET reasons why you expect to attain and maintain such a price at the volumes proposed. This may, in certain cases, require some analysis of customer sensitivity to price, relative to both the quality of the product as well as to alternatives. It is not, however, always so easy. The price which Malise Graham is charging may seem rather high to you, but what do you base your judgement upon? Is it other containers? Is it the fact that it is wood rather than polystyrene? Is it the quality of the leaflet? Is it the fact that you do not like paying so much money for a mail-order product? Alternatively, Tom Wills' process reduces the cost of brake linings, but should it reduce the price? Whatever you finally decide, any evidence of customer reaction through sales already made will be very valuable in convincing any potential investor of the saleability, and thus credibility, of both your product and its price.

2. *Promotion*

Just as marketing is not only selling, so promotion is not only advertising. It covers any activity which is aimed at encouraging the potential customers to buy your product. In other words it includes such choices as:

(a) Attending trade fairs: an important source of business for Eurobond.
(b) Offering discounts for bulk purchase.
(c) Obtaining free editorials and comment in journals, newspapers and possibly on television: see how useful this was for Pam Murphy.
(d) Designing effective packaging: the brochure was the product for Lingua Franca.
(e) Deciding whether to employ a sales force, use agents or be responsible for customer contact and liaison yourself: a fundamental question for PEI.
(f) Sponsorship: such as that provided by Cyril Fletcher for Pamal.

Even if advertising is an important part of your strategy, remember that there are other media as well as the expensive national newspapers or television. These include descriptive leaflets, inserts for trade journals, business cards, posters on hoardings or in buses, point of sale material or direct mail. Whatever you decide, the message and the medium must fit the product. Ask yourself if you were placing advertisements for the Omniclock, Hi-fi, Girogift or a new language school, would you have chosen those described? Finally do not forget that your letter headings are an important method of advertising your company.

Whatever mix you choose, your investor will be looking for evidence that you have very clearly focused your promotional activity on your potential customers. Lavish advertising campaigns do not necessarily impress. On the other hand a 'small ad' even in the right trade journal, would not be appropriate for a new, expensive and complex technical product such as the Slurrimaster. Even if your potential customers saw it, they would be unlikely to take it seriously.

3. Product

This will already have been dealt with earlier in your proposal, but it is perhaps worth underlining again the way in which your particular product or process fits customer needs, through such factors as appearance, accessories and other service elements, or range of sizes.

4. Place

'Place' is about channels of distribution. Do you intend to use retailers, wholesalers, agents or will you sell direct to the customer? Tom Wills has decided to avoid head-on competition by selling his brake linings through the retail, replacement market. This clearly reduces his potential market and the credibility of his product whilst at the same time possibly increasing his profit margin. David Jones, on the other hand, is not absolutely clear whether he is selling a timepiece, a curiosity or a furnishing item. Therefore, the question of whether the Omniclock should be sold through jewellery shops, gift shops, or high-design furniture shops, such as Heals, remains very much open. Having decided what is an appropriate channel, you must then show any evidence which you have that your chosen intermediaries are, in fact, prepared to handle your product and to give it whatever attention it may need? If you are dealing with a highly sophisticated technical product or process, such as the Slurrimaster, you also need to decide who will be responsible for repair and service? If it is to be your channels, are they aware of this and are they, indeed, competent?

As has been emphasised constantly, you must demonstrate in your proposal that the method chosen clearly matches the product characteristics. The investor must be convinced that you have explored the various options appropriate and that the one you have chosen is likely to be successful. Therefore, a list of potential customers and/or channels is encouraging. A record of sales actually made and a note from a satisfied customer is strong evidence of both a product tested in the market and your commitment. This does have one proviso – the customer must be credible. He must either be a well-known figure to the potential investor or be demonstrably active in your chosen market. Data like this are reasonably easy to obtain in technical or industrial markets, such as those of Light Engineering, PEI or Eurobond Laminates, where the customers are other industrial companies and tend to be relatively few in number. For the consumer market, evidence that a successful retailer is prepared to allocate shelf space to your product shows that he believes that it has sales potential.

Included with your choice of channels should also be some indication of your chosen methods of distribution. Do you intend to use post, rail, containers or lorries? Are there any particular problems of security or safety? Will this imply that you need special types of carriers? Are they readily available and will this be a substantial part of your product cost? Many of the difficulties in pricing and distribution faced by Pamal are a function of the expensive distribution channels chosen.

The above questions apply even more so if you intend to export, since safety regulations vary according to country. Notice the complexity, and thus the risks, associated with exporting hi-fi to Yugoslavia as well as with Girogift both of which on the surface seem very simple ideas. As with all questions concerning exports, unless you have a specific expertise, it is worth taking professional advice on dealing with all the regulations, requirements and legislation, and indicating how far you have got in your proposal. However, a note of warning: unless your product is inherently international, your investor will expect you to demonstrate that you can establish your company at home before launching on an export drive.

Production Strategy

One of the major difficulties which firms face, particularly during the start-up phase, is the matching of production or capacity to sales. Unsatisfied orders or idle plant and labour are both expensive. Despite this, many proposals ignore any description of how the product will be made, simply concentrating upon arguments to show that a market exists and can be attacked. This is not enough. Your potential investor needs to be convinced that, even allowing for problems, you have designed a production strategy which will match the market strategy already described. It is useful to divide this part of your analysis into two phases, the initial set-up and, say, the first two years of consolidation.

1. The Set-up

This part of your proposal will be concerned primarily with location and size. Location in terms of area and type of property, and size in terms of capacity and labour force. Obviously these may be interlinking, so that, like PEI, you may have chosen a particular area because the necessary skilled labour is available there. You may, like Eurobond

Laminates, be negotiating a particular site or property because it happens to be just the right size and has many of the amenities you require. If you do have a particular property in mind, you should show how far you have gone in negotiating terms and what these terms may be. This will be useful to the investor not only in assessing your commitment but also in reducing the level of uncertainty around any cost and cash-flow forecasts you may produce.

Both for plant and equipment, and for raw-material supplies, you will need to demonstrate availability at the right price and in the right quantities. This applies not only to the traditional manufacturing facility, but also to the various types of service business. The use of University College by Lingua Franca not only adds to the courses' credibility in the customers eyes, but also suggests to the potential investor that a credible teaching institution is prepared to support the business by selling space. You should, however, also point your investor towards any potential problems. For example, if you have only one supplier for a particularly vital item, what contingency plans have you made? More importantly, remember that others cannot read your mind. An important consideration in evaluating Continental Trucking is the availability of return loads. Richard Brown had 'forgotten' to say that he had strong links with an Italian company which imports into the UK!

2. The First Two Years

During the initial stages, you must demonstrate what strategy you intend to adopt to achieve your optimum production and over what time scale. This will imply some idea of, for example, the necessary stock levels or the extent of training or product testing necessary. A critical-path or network diagram inserted here would be useful both as a guide for the investor and as a planning aid for yourself. Moreover, it should force you to check your time estimates carefully. Any time lost in the set-up stage can rarely be recovered and businesses which were inherently profitable when established have failed because poor planning in the early stages has resulted in too heavy a financial drag.

Whatever choices you make in your production strategy, do not pare down your estimates to 'please' your investor. If anything does eventually go wrong which you could have reasonably been expected to forecast, he will trust you far less than if you are realistic to begin with.

The People

So far, this chapter has been about the organisation and testing of the business. Yet we know that without committed people no business can survive. There are many books and research works which attempt to describe the characteristics of a successful entrepreneur but they can be summarised in three words: GOALS, SKILLS and HUNGER. It is a combination of these which all your investors – customers and suppliers as well as bankers – will be looking for.

First there are your GOALS. Quite simply, what are you in it for and how does that translate into a business? Alan Reed, Fred Dean and Mike Schofield believed in their product and wanted more freedom to develop it than they were getting under the umbrella of their employer. The same applies to Mike Ford and Malcolm Evans. Mr Singh and John Clark were opportunists – they wanted to make money. So did Rod Senior and Richard Brown. Tom Wills, on the other hand, whilst he seems to want to make money, could well turn into a perpetual inventor. Equally, Malise Graham is not sure whether he wants to grow a large business or run a small jobbing garden-furniture firm. Whatever you decide will determine the nature of the business you then create. However, if there are others involved, it is even more important to recognise that partners in any marriage can grow apart. Bob Kent and Patrick Thorpe have a common goal in wishing to save Certikin, but will there be other needs which are likely to surface when survival is assured? Will they, and the partners in Light Engineering, suffer the same fate as SFL?

Secondly there are your SKILLS. Is there sufficient strength in the ownership to MAKE, MARKET and MANAGE? Light Engineering, Eurobond Laminates and Certikin would score high here, but what of the rest? And more importantly, how do you judge? Alan Sealey is a skilled turner with no management or even administrative experience. Richard Brown seems to understand the organisational issues, but can he really drive a truck? Your investors will base their judgement on your past experience as well as your inclinations, Robert Barclay has little language teaching experience, but has demonstrably worked hard at the tedious process of putting the business together. Mr Singh, on the other hand, does not appear to have any relevant experience, just a few good contacts. David Jones's experience as a dentist may well demonstrate some management ability but his preoccupation with the Omniclock itself suggests that a second person, either as a partner or an employee, may be needed to translate the product into a business.

Pam Murphy is clearly excellent at marketing as well as product development, but in her case the sheer magnitude of the tasks facing her require other people to be involved. HUNGER comes in many forms – physical, intellectual and emotional. Sometimes it is called courage, dedication, commitment; sometimes it is called sheer pig-headedness. Whichever way you choose to view it, it is clear that the single-minded determination of the hungry entrepreneur will sweep away, or ignore, all the difficulties which will inevitably face him. He will simply never accept 'no' as an answer.

The Money

In this section the investor will expect to see an outline of the financial viability of the proposed project. This will require four types of statement:

1. Profit and loss forecasts.
2. Pro-forma balance sheets.
3. Cash-flow forecasts.
4. Break-even analyses.

The RELIABILITY of all these will obviously vary according to both the availability of good data and your ability to forecast timing. So, for example, you may be completely accurate in forecasting the level of your first month's sales, but inaccurate in estimating your launch date. This could seriously affect your cash flows. Therefore, it is important to indicate the areas which are likely to be SENSITIVE to change and produce alternative financial analyses, otherwise known as sensitivity tests. It should be noted, however, that too much data is as bad as too little. Therefore you should confine yourself to one or two significant factors.

Any forecast is likely to be more unreliable the further into the future which you project. This is even more the case for a new company, with a new product, which is possibly competing in a new market. Nevertheless, the investor will need some idea of the likely profitability of the exercise over a reasonable investment period. Ideally he would like you to see, at a minimum, forecasts for the first two years, broken down into quarterly or monthly statements, whichever is appropriate for your business.

If you are unfamiliar with the preparation of these statements, it is important to SEEK PROFESSIONAL ADVICE. Ask your accountant to do it for you. Apart from anything else, this will give you an independent check on the financial viability of the strategy you have chosen. If you do not have an accountant and are serious about the proposition, then you should employ one. If you do have one and he is not prepared to do the analysis for you, then you should change him – he is not going to be much help to you later when you are running your business.

In presenting these statements you will be indicating both to yourself and to your investor:

(a) How much money is needed: the size of the project.
(b) How the money will be spent: on long term assets or working capital.
(c) How profitable the venture will be: both in terms of margins and return on capital.
(d) How risky the venture is likely to be.

More importantly, remember that this is not an artificial exercise, done for the purpose of raising money. It should form the basis of your future management control system. Any variation from it can only be either bad luck or poor judgement. I hope it is not the latter – GOOD LUCK!